MANUFACTURING'S NEW MANDATE

MANUFACTURING'S NEW MANDATE

The Tools for Leadership

DAN CIAMPA
Rath & Strong, Inc.

WILEY

John Wiley & Sons

NEW YORK · CHICHESTER · BRISBANE · TORONTO · SINGAPORE

Library of Congress Cataloging in Publication Data:

Ciampa, Dan.
    Manufacturing's new mandate.

    1. United States—Manufactures—Management.
I. Title.

HD9725.C49   1988   658.4   88–2515
ISBN 0-471-63375-5

Printed in the United States of America

10 9 8 7 6 5 4 3 2 1

This book is dedicated to
SANDY JENKS,
a strong but gentle giver who helped
launch a thousand careers

Preface

American manufacturers today are facing tough challenges on every front:

- Foreign competitors want increasing shares of markets traditionally dominated by U.S. companies—and some are winning them hands down.
- Customers demand more and better service, just-in-time delivery, and flawless quality.
- Employees seek more control over problem solving and decision making.
- The need for individual initiative and more innovation has spawned a resurgence in creativity programs and a push toward in-house entrepreneurial training.

At the same time, there is increasing pressure to create a common vision that every employee can relate to and companywide norms that lead to consistent behavior across departments.

Through all of this run complaints that U.S. industrial leaders are shortsighted. Wall Street, however, still measures success in the short term.

These challenges must be attacked through simultaneous and coordinated actions which constitute the leader's agenda. American manufacturers find themselves in a world of paradoxes that only a leader who can balance vision, strength, and sensitivity will be able to sort out: containing cost while improving quality; improving customer service while reducing inventory; doing everything as the customer wants it the first time while dramatically cutting lead times.

Meeting these challenges requires a leader who can balance priorities that seem contradictory, balance firmness with flexibility, evidence strong leadership while caring for the needs of others, make tough decisions with willingness to push decision-making power lower in the organization.

In the 1950s and early 1960s, the emphasis of American manufacturing was on cost control. Productivity meant getting costs as low as possible and pushing people to produce more and faster. This was the heyday of industrial engineering which offered work measurement and individual incentives.

In the late 1960s and through much of the 1970s, the information era was born. Leaders of manufacturing companies were told that being more systematic, data driven, and analytical was necessary. Massive and expensive information systems were created and forced into American companies in the hope that they would bring more profits. What resulted too often was complexity and alienation.

In the late 1970s and early 1980s, leaders of manufacturing companies saw foreign competitors become stronger at a frightening pace. Many thought that human error and labor costs were the culprits. They were told that the answer was automation. In recent years, even leaders of companies that poured huge amounts of money, time, and energy into computer-based manufacturing have agreed that automation is a lot tougher than it first appeared and that it is hardly the cure for all manufacturing ills.

American manufacturing leaders are beginning to real-ize that there is no one program that will do all that is needed, that it is likely that a combination of tools and tech-niques is best, and that many of the solutions of yesterday may bring marginal results today and tomorrow. The fact is that the marketplace has changed and, most of all, the ex-pectations of the customer have changed.

In short, the power of the customer has increased dra-matically. The customer wants flawless quality and delivery often and on time. What the last decade has proven is that this is not unreasonable and that if one company cannot satisfy those requirements, another will—even if it makes its product half a world away.

The good news is that the tools and techniques to do the job are available. They are coming from two directions.

The first is from the discipline of quality as it has devel-oped over the last 50 years. In addition, there has been a dramatic change in the last decade in the way the tools of quality are applied. Those tools are no longer used to detect problems that exist, but rather to prevent problems from happening in the first place. This re-orientation has brought some rather profound changes in the practice and ushered in something that has come to be called Total Quality.

The second direction is from Just-in-Time, a set of seven tools and techniques that can bring truly astounding im-provements in lead time, flexibility, and costs.

It is the right combination of Total Quality and Just-in-Time that can set the stage for the appropriate elements of computer-integrated manufacturing technology.

The bad news is that the culture that exists in many companies (the norms and the way things are done) and, in particular, their organizational climate (the particular environment of the company, which has a great impact on people's motivation) do not support Total Quality and Just-in-Time. It is not that the tools and techniques are not applicable; rather, it is that some companies just cannot seem to make them work. The major reasons for this failure are that in these companies people are not working as a team, do not share a compelling vision of what the future can hold, and are not committed to the changes that must take place.

In order to implement changes in the magnitude and at the depth needed, people at every level of the organization must be committed to making those changes work. This is where the leader comes in.

The leader does not have control over employees' commitment. However, the leader can create the sort of climate that is conducive to positive change and to employees becoming committed to making it happen. If the leader can accomplish this task, his or her company will have a head start toward being much more competitive and making products and services truly world class.

This book is about how a leader of a manufacturing company can rise to the challenges the company faces and move that company toward becoming a manufacturing leader.

It is about personal challenges as well as corporate challenges. It focuses on what leaders must do to understand and to change their own behavior in order to establish a climate within the organization so that successful, competitive, world-class manufacturing can take place.

There are an increasing number of books on Total Quality, Just-in-Time, and Computer Integrated Manufacturing. Most admit that there is a people/organizational climate piece to the puzzle that must fit into place, but they stop at that point and go on to describe the technical pieces without going into any depth on how to involve people, change the climate, and make sure changes last. None addresses the unique needs of the key player in this picture—the leader.

While my colleague, Ed Hay, in his book *The Just-in-Time Breakthrough* (Wiley, 1988), has shown how to carry out the mechanics of a transition to a Just-in-Time manufacturing environment, this book focuses on what the leader must do to make sure that technical, management, and attitudinal changes take place so that both Total Quality and Just-in-Time can be viable.

Only a strong, confident, and sensitive leader can prepare an organization to do what needs to be done. The job involves developing a vision that all members of the organization can share, giving enough control to managers to solve day-to-day problems, yet retaining control of the long-range thinking, planning, and strategy to make sure the transition does not lose momentum—especially in the first critical months and years.

Only this sort of leader can break down the myriad "people barriers" that stand in the way of making radical change in an organization and do it in such a way that the climate becomes more positive and people commit themselves to continuous improvement.

In order to develop this strength and ability, the leader must be willing to critically look at himself, the people he has put around him, the systems that have been developed, and the way he exerts his influence. He must not only understand the situation the company faces and know what options are available, but also look carefully at his own values, attitudes, and leadership style, and how these can affect the way he makes decisions and deals with people.

Finally, once the changes have been made, the leader must develop ways to "codify" those changes, to change measurement and reward systems so they better match the realities the company is facing and the behavior expected of employees.

The message should be clear: in times of rapid change it is not enough for a leader to be a fireman, willing and able to make fast decisions of a reactive nature. A leader today must increasingly take the long view, must be able to spot changes in the business environment before they happen, and must, with great sensitivity, guide the entire organization to change in order to face new market demands.

That is the leader's challenge.

DAN CIAMPA

Lexington, Massachusetts
March 1988

Acknowledgments

The beliefs and experience condensed in this book are the product of consulting with a long list of clients in projects that were both very successful and, in some cases, not as successful as they should have been; both have held tremendous potential for learning. They are also the product of my own experience as a manager and then a leader trying to alter an organization climate and usher in a new era to meet new needs.

The primary conclusion from the last 20 years in both my role as consultant and as leader is that the task of bringing about change in a positive way is neither easy nor something about which to be glib. Machiavelli said in *The Prince,* ". . . there is nothing more difficult to carry out nor more doubtful of success, nor dangerous to handle, than to initiate a new order of things. For the reformer has enemies in all those who profit by the old order, and only lukewarm defenders in all those who would profit by the new. . . . partly from the incredulity of mankind who do not truly believe in anything until they have had actual experience of it."

These words express the situation of many leaders trying to bring about change. I am not particularly a fan of Machiavelli; we would disagree violently on how to deal with that sort of situation—him by politics and in an adversarial way, me through getting issues out on the table and striving first for trust and finding common ground.

John Kennedy had something to say on the subject as well, "The credit belongs to the man who is actually in the arena, whose face is marred by dust and sweat and blood; a man who knows the great enthusiasms and the great devotions, who spends himself in a worthy cause; who in the end, knows the triumph of high achievement, and if he fails at least fails while daring greatly, so that his place shall never be with those cold and timid souls, who know neither victory nor defeat."

This book is for those of us who are in the middle (between the enemies and the lukewarm defenders) and in the arena. The leaders who have put themselves on the line and are committed to bringing about something better.

Through the years, friends and colleagues have been both sounding boards for ideas and helpful critics—Dave Berlew, Jim Richard, John Burns, Tom Thomson, Arthur Turner, and Bruce Henderson stand out in this regard. Ed Hay and Joe Juran have contributed technical pieces to the puzzle and Tom Woods has contributed to problem-solving techniques in Chapter 2. Jon Zonderman's help has been immeasurable in preparing this manuscript—his ability to make clear what is complex is second only to his empathy and listening skills. Meredith Allen and Debbie Sarajian have been patient and flexible, ensuring that all the pieces fall into place.

It has been my clients who have contributed most to the ideas and tools in this book. They have provided the opportunity to put these ideas to work and have given the feedback necessary to adjust and refine. Some of the clients who stand out are Dave Harrington of Delta Rubber, Ed Fogarty

Acknowledgments

of Corning, Ron Cotman of General Electric, Tom Soper of Alexander & Alexander, Tom Vanderslice, Roland Pampel, and Frank Faggiano of Apollo Computer, George Raymond of Raymond Corp., Richard Bovender of RJR/Archer, Mike Lorelli and Ron Tidmore of Pepsi, Ginny Ward and Bob Eichinger of Pillsbury, Chris Letts and Mark Chesnut of Cummins Engine, and Ed Alkire of Air Products.

None of this would have much meaning if it weren't for Elaine and Devon, who have been supportive and understanding through many years when my work has not allowed us to be together.

D.C.

Contents

Contents

Contents

Chapter 1

The CEO's Challenge

A friend who runs a medium-sized job shop called one day and said, "I really need some help. Last Wednesday a customer called and asked that we quote on some new business. The company is a relatively new customer for us, and buys a lot of the kind of product we provide from two of our largest competitors. We got our foot in the door a few months ago and since then have been trying to show them what we can really do."

"Have you shown them?" I asked.

"Yes, but that's the problem. After the call I spoke to the vice president of sales and marketing. I told him to call the customer right away and get detailed specs, then speak to the vice president of engineering and development to get a quote back quickly.

"The next day I asked the marketing vice president if he had called the customer yet. He said he hadn't but would get on it right away. On Friday afternoon, the vice president of marketing told me he had indeed called the customer and spoken to my engineering vice president, but the engineering people thought the product was very complex and would need some time to get a quote together.

"I called in the vice presidents of marketing, engineering, and manufacturing, and they told me why this part could not be made—it was too hard to make, tolerances were too tight. The customer doesn't guarantee a large order. We would own the mold. Tooling costs would be high. They said we're backed up in product development as is, there aren't enough people to do everything, and the customer has been a pain in the neck on the part we're currently running for him. He's trying to squeeze us on deliveries and quality, trying to get the product faster and better.

"Can you imagine, listing all those reasons why we

shouldn't satisfy the customer? I read them the riot act, told them to get that customer a quote by Tuesday morning, even if they had to work all weekend to do it! The quote got there Tuesday morning. On Wednesday morning, one week after the initial request, I followed up.

"The customer said that when he didn't hear from us by Thursday afternoon, he called a competitor, a Korean company that had just opened up an operation in town. They had an engineer and a regional sales manager in the customer's offices that afternoon, and their quote was on his desk Friday at noon. The specs he had given my marketing vice president Friday afternoon had come from the specs given to him by the Korean company a few hours earlier.

"We were outhustled by a hungry, sharp competitor. That's why we need help."

This tale is frequently heard, with minor variations. Before they even deliver their quote to the customer, American manufacturing companies are getting beaten by their own lack of response to customer needs and often by their inability to maintain quality in their products after they are awarded contracts.

There is no one problem that plagues American business, and there is no one button to push for a solution. Most manufacturing businesses have a whole set of problems, some in technical areas, some in behavioral areas, and some in the area of leadership. Problems may present themselves in stark terms or, as in this example, appear as a general malaise throughout the company.

Technical problems are most apparent. When Western manufacturers call in consulting help, the symptoms they present are most often in technical areas.

The *cause* of the problem can be quite different from the *symptoms* that lead the patient to seek help. Familiar symptoms seen on an initial visit to a manufacturing facility that complains of technical problems are outmoded floor layouts, misused technology, poor performance standards, or manufacturing data that are not organized or accessible. Companies that display such visible technical or physical problems are usually also plagued by behavioral and leadership problems, and their effect is to prevent the technical problems from being solved.

Each set of issues in this troika of problems facing Western manufacturing can be solved. We have the tools: *Total Quality* (TQ), *Just-in-Time* (JIT), and *Computer Integrated Manufacturing* (CIM). But success in using these tools requires using them well and understanding the logic of how they can be used together. They are powerful when they are instituted in the proper order, at the proper time, and under the proper circumstances.

Top management needs to remember two paramount rules in approaching these problems:

1. Never assume that chronic technical problems can be overcome without resolving behavioral and/or leadership problems as well.
2. Changes made in one of the three problem areas will inevitably cause disequilibrium and may necessitate further changes in the other areas.

The three problem areas—technical, behavior, and leadership—must be dealt with in reverse order. This is what I call the *Y Principle:* Success of new technologies means implementing changes in the way work gets done, overcoming behavioral barriers, and exhibiting creative, able, and sensitive leadership (see Figure 1–1).

First, let me define how the terms technical, behavioral, and leadership are used here.

- *Technical:* Designing a new layout (for a plant or cell), developing new software, designing new equipment and work processes or protocols or standards, providing for the physical and technical tools/ techniques that will be used. Some technical tools include Manufacturing Resource Planning (MRP II), Manufacturing Automation Protocol (MAP), robots, Computer Aided Design (CAD), Computer Aided Manufacturing (CAM), and Statistical Process Control (SPC).
- *Behavioral:* How people work in groups and communicate within their group and with other groups. How they influence each other and negotiate to get work accomplished.
- *Leadership:* An ability for developing and describing a common vision of how things could be, establishing a strategy to get there, creating the right work

Figure 1–1
The Y-Principle

environment, operating and making decisions at a high ethical and business level; and doing all this in such a way that people are willing to follow, but at the same time making sure that the right people are in the right slots and, in particular, setting high standards.

To make technical changes of the magnitude needed in most U.S. companies and, more importantly, to enable those changes to last, employee behavior must change. Before employee behavior can change, attitudes must change, and before that can happen, the leader must ensure a climate that is supportive and that encourages attitude changes. The leader must be firmly committed to the kinds of behavioral and technical changes that need to be made. Technical changes require different behaviors in an environment of less compartmentalization and more cooperation which are necessary for the success of technical innovations such as set up reduction, pull scheduling systems, SPC, and MRP II.

To deal with these issues, a company's executive officer must understand three things:

1. The realities of manufacturing in today's world, and the type of environment necessary to deal with today's challenges.
2. The relationships required between departments in a modern manufacturing company and the barriers to be overcome for effective interactions, including the biases of each department head because of previous experience and training.
3. His own personal leadership style, its strengths and weaknesses, and how to set up superstructures that complement the strengths and compensate for the weaknesses.

REALITIES

The realities of manufacturing in the late 1980s and early 1990s will require leaders who are far different from those of previous decades.

Twenty years ago, manufacturers traded off low inventory for high customer response in the belief that to be responsive to customers high levels of inventory had to be maintained. The problem with this philosophy is that high inventories not only drive up costs—either forcing price pressure or squeezing margins—but also hide a multitude of other problems that adversely affect meeting customer needs.

Today most people believe the opposite is true: to be truly responsive to customer needs, a manufacturer should have small inventories, small product runs, and the ability to change over a manufacturing line quickly.

Skills akin to those of a high-wire act are needed to balance today's manufacturing and marketplace needs:

- Low inventory and high customer response.
- Low product cost and high quality.
- Low operating cost and high training and retraining.
- Low bureaucracy and high effectiveness and control.
- Low supplier base and high reliability of supply.
- Low risk profile and high entrepreneurial behavior.

In the 1960s and 1970s, the preferred solutions were to lower direct labor costs and create information systems. The thought was that manufacturing leaders needed data, needed to have their businesses run more systematically. The area of Inventory and Production Control developed because of the belief that the key to success was knowing where things were, where they were supposed to go, how much they cost, and how they would be controlled.

Cost control was a synonym for lowering labor costs, and that meant getting rid of people. In his 1986 *Harvard Business Review* article, "The Productivity Paradox," Wickham Skinner expressed his concern:

The emphasis on direct costs, which attends the productivity focus, leads a company to use management controls that focus on the wrong targets. Inevitably, these controls key on direct labor: overhead is allocated by direct labor; variances from standards are calculated from direct labor. Performance in customer service, delivery, lead times, quality, and asset turns are secondary. The reward system based on such controls drives behavior toward simplistic goals that represent only a small fraction of total costs while the real costs lie in overhead and purchased materials.

Current realizations are that labor must be a partner with management in improvement, that systems are not the entire answer, and that information must go hand-in-hand with a different organizational climate. Success is not a matter of systems but of the people who use them and the environment within which those people work. Systems break down, but if the manufacturing environment changes, change can be lasting.

A common sign hanging on an office wall in a materials or MIS department is shown in Figure 1–2. Such humor

Figure 1–2
The Typical System Lifecycle

Phase 1: Wild Enthusiasm
Phase 2: Disillusionment
Phase 3: Total Confusion
Phase 4: Search for the Guilty
Phase 5: Pass the Buck
Phase 6: Punish the Innocent
Phase 7: Promote the Nonparticipant

usually brings knowing nods and smiles from anyone who has been involved with installing an information system. Sadly, by the late 1970s most companies *expected* problems with system installations and spent millions of dollars and even more valuable man years preparing for the inevitable frustrations.

That kind of wheel spinning will not do. Companies must concentrate on changes that are seen by everyone involved as being real, and as having a possibility of solving the problems that deter excellent work and customer satisfaction.

A commonly used analogy of rocks in a pond is attributed to the Japanese. As shown in Figure 1–3, the level of the water in the pond (inventory) is lowered in order to expose the rocks (problems) so that these problems can be examined and solved.

A corollary to the analogy of the pond water and the rocks applies to people problems rather than technical problems (Figure 1–4). The water in this case is the organizational culture, which often covers up people problems (the

Figure 1–3
The Realities of Manufacturing

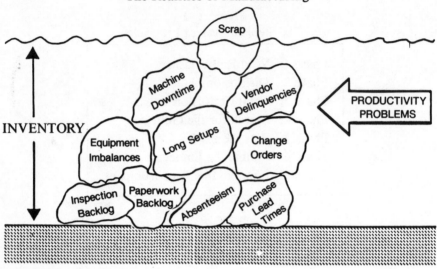

Figure 1–4
People-Related Problems in Manufacturing

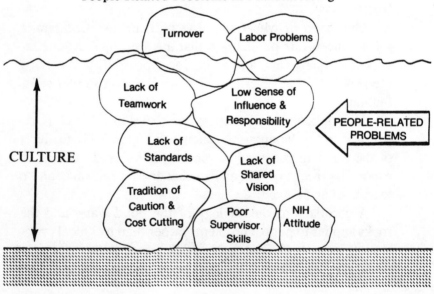

rocks), or at least causes managers to see people problems somewhat differently when they are "under water."

The solution here is not as easy as for technical problems. The organizational culture cannot be siphoned off like the inventory level. Managers need to develop a way to see things as they are, to act as divers, going into the murky water with special gear (specially designed surveys of an organization's climate) to see clearly where the rocks are and be able to help the company negotiate around them or eliminate them.

What particular kind of work environment will meet today's needs? One that encourages participation so people feel involved in the way the business is run. One that rewards teamwork and discourages divisive behavior. One that ensures that trouble signs are recognized before major problems appear, and that people take responsibility to avoid problems or, if already unavoidable, solve them. The environment must stress doing the right things in the right way even more than "doing it right the first time" and must foster a feeling of self-confidence among employees so that they believe they have influence over changing what is around them.

One of the first changes that must come about in the manufacturing environment is in the relationships between people *within* the company.

INTERDEPENDENT RELATIONSHIPS

The relationships between departments in a manufacturing business are terribly important. Too often, those relationships show not only a lack of knowledge about what the other departments do but a lack of caring.

In the past, most companies were allowed or encouraged to grow in a compartmentalized way, where communication was vertical and barriers between departments were so common that they were expected; walking from one department to another was often like seeing different companies under the same roof. (See Figure 1–5.) This was true because of the prevailing concept of running a manufacturing company.

Figure 1–5
Communication Barriers

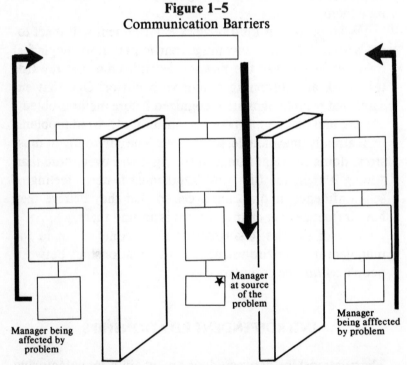

Because of "walls" between departments, communication (arrows) goes up to the leader then down into another department rather than across at the mid-manager level where the issues originate and should be solved.

The way people believed it was best to make product led to these operating characteristics.

There is a growing realization that there must be a better way. Implementing changes necessary to bring high quality, low cost, and satisfied customers today requires coordination between departments. Coordination requires teamwork, which means cross-departmental communications, common goals, and collaborative relationships.

Product design is an example of a need for close work among engineering, manufacturing, and marketing. People in engineering often do not fully understand the impact of their design changes on those who must manufacture the product. Those in manufacturing do not fully realize that how well they meet design specifications has an impact on how tightly designed future products are.

What has developed in Western manufacturing is a circle of distrust that perpetuates itself: The engineers do not trust the manufacturing managers or employees to meet specifications; therefore, they make the specifications tighter than needed. The manufacturing people, at the same time, know that the design specifications are more rigid than necessary, and consequently don't feel compelled to meet them consistently.

The marketing and sales people think the engineers are too far removed from the reality of the marketplace and what the customer wants, while the engineers believe the salespeople will do anything for a sale, and the marketing people do not know the technology and want everything developed and completed yesterday. This sort of relationship is shown in Figure 1–6.

A pattern of going to the brink of conflict and then backing off extends well into the senior management group.

Figure 1–6
Interdepartmental Communication May Not Be Clear

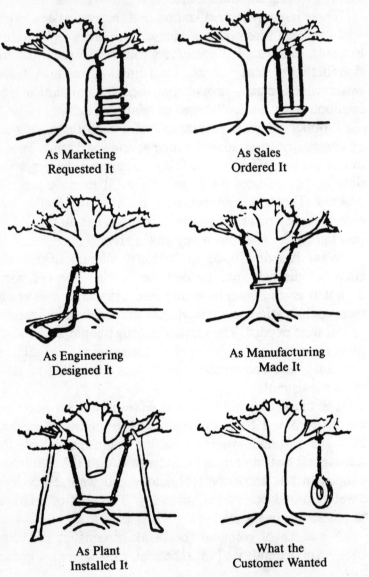

As Marketing
Requested It

As Sales
Ordered It

As Engineering
Designed It

As Manufacturing
Made It

As Plant
Installed It

What the
Customer Wanted

If the vice president of engineering is always at odds with his counterpart in manufacturing, one can hardly expect breakthroughs in interpersonal relationships between engineers and production people.

In addition, few CEOs or other top managers of manufacturing companies or divisions come from the ranks of manufacturing—only about 20 percent, according to a recent survey. Some top management, but not a majority, come from engineering. A number come from marketing and financial areas.

The relationships between departments in most Western manufacturing companies as they are constituted today, rather than preventing problems, may actually *cause* many problems. Bad relationships between engineering and manufacturing, or between marketing and manufacturing, emphasize what technical, quality, and delivery problems exist and keep them from being solved.

Although technical and quality problems appear as overt symptoms, they are often signs of deeper, more systemic problems that must be diagnosed and cured before the technical problems permanently disappear. This is where the leadership part of the Y Principle comes in.

LEADERSHIP STYLE

Understanding what leadership is and what leadership style a top manager has is an important step in problem solving in modern manufacturing companies.

When it comes to widescale organizational change, good effective leadership is different from the myth of good leadership as personified by General Patton or John Wayne.

This mythical notion of leadership is inadequate in the complex, manufacturing world.

The effective leader asks questions more than he makes declarative statements. The leader is not the person with all the answers, but rather provides an environment in which employees feel responsible and rewarded for coming up with their own answers. How the leader accomplishes this with his particular leadership style, in large part, determines his success. This in no way is meant to imply that only one style achieves these end results. That is why it is important to have some way to analyze a leader's style.

In the late 1970s, I became familiar with the work of Alex George, a political scientist at Stanford University. He had studied the personal leadership styles of American presidents. The more I delved into the research of George and others on this topic, the more convinced I was that these models could be used by my clients, who were leaders of businesses, to better understand their impact and to help them lead more effectively. Data are available about what goes on in the Oval Office (in fact we know more about what goes on in the Oval Office than in most corporate executive suites) and the results of decisions made by this highly visible leader are apparent, often quickly.

Personal leadership style and the impact it has on bringing about change in a manufacturing company will be discussed in detail in Chapter 4.

It is important for a leader to understand his particular style of leadership, what its strengths and weaknesses are, what will complement his particular style, and what impact his leadership style will have on decision making and problem solving in the company.

There are four basic steps in the problem-solving, decision-making process:

1. Defining the issues
2. Defining the options
3. Choosing an option
4. Implementing the selection.

The point at which a leader enters the problem-solving, decision-making process has a lot to do with how he manages it and what results are achieved. Some leaders want to enter the process at Step 1 and stay with it through all four steps (Jimmy Carter had this style), while others do not enter the process until Step 3 (more the style of Ronald Reagan). How successful an individual is often depends on whether his preferred style is complemented or matched by the right support staff and whether he is operating in a system that presents information in the best way for that style.

Usually, when a leader calls me and says, "Things just are not going well, decisions are falling through the cracks, problems are remaining unsolved, I need help," the issue has less to do with the leader himself than with how he is managing the problem-solving, decision-making process. More often than not, the leader has not determined how best to fit his personal style to the process itself. For example, he may be entering at Step 2, trying to formulate options. It may be that this individual is better at evaluating the options (Step 3) rather than formulating them. In Chapter 4, this will be discussed in more detail.

The key is to understand the leader's personal leadership style and its impact on problem solving and decision making. The leader must develop the proper superstructure of people and systems to support that leadership style and assist in making the decisions that need to be made.

Today's leader is a social engineer and a corporate climate engineer. He or she must provide an atmosphere in which people are rewarded for behaving supportively and appropriately within the system. Employee behavior cannot be changed by merely telling people they need to change their behavior. Nor can behavior be changed by offering to pay more. The leader, and his team, must find ways to effectively communicate through words and deeds that changes are imperative to professional and personal success.

For people to change their behavior, they must change their attitudes. To do this, they need the following:

- An understanding of the need to change
- A belief that it is important to change
- A belief that the leaders want change
- A belief that they will receive help in making the change
- A belief that they will be rewarded for changing
- An understanding of what life will be like with change
- A compelling picture of how things will be
- Confidence that they have or will have the skills needed to change
- A belief that life will be better in meaningful ways after the change
- A belief that needs will be met.

How the leader creates the environment for such thoughts, beliefs, and feelings will go a long way toward promoting behavior changes within the organization.

CHALLENGE

The leader's challenge can be stated simply: to respond to the demands of today's marketplace. However, this seemingly simple challenge is complicated by a whole host of corollary challenges to the leader.

In responding to today's challenges, the leader must not repeat past mistakes, either his or those of the manufacturing world in general. The business world today is far less forgiving than in the past, and mistakes are more easily fatal.

The leader must thoroughly understand the tools and techniques that can be used to make his company's environment better suited to today's manufacturing and business realities. Those tools must be implemented in such a way that the people using them will be committed to continuous improvement.

Finally, they must be implemented in such a way that the leader can get up and face himself or herself in the morning, knowing that the decisions made were ethical, that is, the decisions were not made merely for expedient "business" reasons, but were in the best interests of the business as a collection of people.

Without tackling the issue of business ethics, let me emphasize that ethics is an important consideration for the leader when making the cultural changes necessary to successfully implement total quality, just in time, and computer integrated manufacturing (TQ, JIT, and CIM).

In this technological age, we are at great risk of giving up our moral superstructure, within which we need to operate and make decisions. We must watch out for the ten deadly sins of the technological age:

- Business without morality
- Politics without principle
- Science without humanity
- Pleasure without conscience
- Wealth without work
- Knowledge without character
- Work without contribution
- Education without reality
- Achievement without humility
- Excellence without modesty.

The next 12 chapters are designed to help leaders understand TQ, JIT, and CIM, the roles they can play in helping a company achieve manufacturing excellence, and the way they can be successfully and morally implemented.

Chapter 2

TQ/JIT/CIM:
Partners, Not Competitors

Total Quality; Just-in-Time; Computer Integrated Manufacturing—different sounding phrases that are shorthand for some powerful, modern management tools.

Each one is quite different. The goal of *Total Quality* (TQ) is to make sure that each step in the process of making a product or providing a service—in fact, every activity that is done in any business—is done correctly, the first time. *Just-in-Time* (JIT) asks that operation 1 not be done until operation 2 needs the product that operation 1 will make, that each operation complete its activity "just-in-time" to move the finished goods down the line, one at a time. *Computer Integrated Manufacturing* (CIM) is the continuation of computerized processes and automation that has become a part of manufacturing since the 1960s, and stresses the integration of the various systems that provide information for decision making throughout the business.

Taken individually, each of these tools has its strengths. Taken together, they can become the most powerful set of tools to propel Western manufacturing forward to become better than ever before.

While TQ, JIT, and CIM can be a powerful team, they are often seen as competing processes. This is not the case; these techniques are not naturally competitors or mutually exclusive. The philosophies of each are not competitive either. What has made TQ, JIT, and CIM competitors is simply that they have been seen as individual entities, and each time a company has explored ways to increase its manufacturing performance, constituencies have formed around each set of techniques, presenting it as *the way* to accomplish the goal. It was believed that a choice had to be made—only one tool could provide the solution—that, in fact, there was only one correct solution to a problem of inadequate manufacturing performance.

This could not be farther from the truth. The only real solution to the malaise of Western manufacturing is an attempt to put together what I call the *Modern Integrated Manufacturing* (MIM) package. That package is shown graphically in Figure 2–1.

Figure 2–1
Modern Integrated Manufacturing Pyramid (MIM Pyramid)

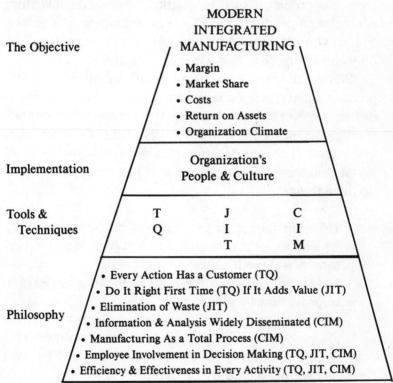

The Objective	**MODERN INTEGRATED MANUFACTURING** • Margin • Market Share • Costs • Return on Assets • Organization Climate
Implementation	Organization's People & Culture
Tools & Techniques	T J C Q I I T M
Philosophy	• Every Action Has a Customer (TQ) • Do It Right First Time (TQ) If It Adds Value (JIT) • Elimination of Waste (JIT) • Information & Analysis Widely Disseminated (CIM) • Manufacturing As a Total Process (CIM) • Employee Involvement in Decision Making (TQ, JIT, CIM) • Efficiency & Effectiveness in Every Activity (TQ, JIT, CIM)

ORIGIN OF MIM

Before we look closely at the MIM pyramid, we will look briefly at the history of this comprehensive thesis about the tools that go into successful manufacturing.

In 1981, I began searching for a unified concept for manufacturing improvement. This was after ten years of experience at Rath & Strong, where we had worked on a case-by-case basis with companies to merge the tools of changing the organizational culture with those of solving technical problems such as quality, production/inventory control, and productivity. This was something of a revolution in consulting, and we are still, to my knowledge, the only consulting firm that uses this approach.

We expanded our scope of multidisciplinary quality problem solving to include prevention-based thinking. In addition, we worked at changing the organization climate through diagnosis and through involvement of employees at every level. This combination is what *Total Quality* is all about, and we set out to develop a TQ approach that would do three things:

- Help clients get to the point where the process by which they were providing services or products to customers was predictable.
- Help clients get into the habit of looking for ways to improve how they did things.
- Get to the root causes of quality problems rather than always dealing with the results or the symptoms. This meant identifying the basic tools that could be used and getting people to use them.

In 1982, I began learning about CIM in a thorough way. The deeper I delved into CIM, the more I became concerned that clients I saw getting into CIM were not ready for it, and that CIM itself had a long way to go to be a practical, cost-efficient tool that was acceptable to employees. Mistakes were still being made, only faster, and processes were being automated that should not have been happening in the first place.

I was also convinced that most CEOs did not really understand what they were getting into as they launched into CIM, just as most did not know what they were getting into in the 1960s and 1970s when they launched into material requirements planning (MRP) efforts. There was just too much to do to get ready for CIM; too much of a leap was needed from the way companies were currently manufacturing in this country.

I knew that prevention-based quality, rather than detection-based, was part of the answer, and that changing the climate to encourage more employee participation was another part, but something was still missing.

The missing piece turned out to be *Just-in-Time* (JIT). The JIT way of manufacturing is clearly suited particularly well to the needs of U.S. business for a number of reasons:

- JIT shares the same philosophical tenets as Total Quality.
- JIT can have an enormous impact on productivity and costs, by reducing waste and unnecessary steps in the production process.
- JIT is particularly amenable to employee involvement, and it works best in a participative, give-and-take sort of climate.

- All but one of JIT's basic elements were quite familiar to people in the United States.
- When done in the right way, JIT offers a low cost/no cost alternative to some of the applications that CIM had been forced into.

If the claims of JIT's potential were accurate, could it be that what was needed to help American manufacturing was a combination of TQ and JIT? It was possible that gains from that combination could set the proper atmosphere for further progress from CIM. As we at Rath and Strong worked on this through the mid-1980s in a number of TQ and JIT implementation projects, it became apparent that a logical sequence of improvement was possible and that one set of tools and techniques had a certain dependence on another.

In 1983, I came up with the notion of Modern Integrated Manufacturing which begins with the premise that Total Quality should provide a base of a predictable process and a climate for innovation and problem solving throughout the entire business. Once that base of TQ is laid, JIT can result in even more impressive savings. In fact, while JIT could be beneficial in just about any circumstance, its greatest potential is when the process is predictable and there is a climate that encourages innovation, teamwork, and problem solving. Once JIT eliminates waste and brings increased flexibility by solving the problems causing these things, the next phase is to capitalize on the potential of CIM through further automation and systems integration, and to gain even more consistency, predictability, and cost reduction. CIM can also then be used to perform the most hazardous tasks.

This model makes sense to us. It can be used in the offices and shop floors of our clients so that the gains can be continuous and employees can take responsibility for improvement.

MIM PYRAMID

Working from the bottom of the pyramid up, it is important to understand that TQ, JIT, and CIM are not manufacturing systems. Rather, they are sets of techniques based on a common philosophy about how manufacturing should be perceived and carried out. Above those three sets of tools and techniques is the umbrella of the organization's climate. Above that are the objectives of modern manufacturing.

In order to have successful Modern Integrated Manufacturing, the objectives first need to be defined, then work must start on the company's organizational climate. The techniques of TQ, JIT, and CIM then need to be instituted in the right sequence. Only if the objectives are clearly defined and the company's climate changed will the conditions be conducive to understanding the philosophical underpinnings of TQ, JIT, and CIM and making the necessary changes for the right reasons.

Without the proper climate, and the proper understanding of the objectives, which together help corporate leaders develop a vision of the company under TQ, JIT, and CIM, the techniques will be instituted for the wrong reason—most often to just cut costs—and will be tried separately, thereby diminishing the power available by combining them.

After this forcing downward through the pyramid, as the techniques of first TQ, then JIT, and finally CIM are implemented, true manufacturing excellence percolates back up through the pyramid; changes in the company's climate really take hold and the objectives make more sense as they are met.

It seems that the best way to comprehend the totality of Modern Integrated Manufacturing is first to understand the objectives, the new realities of the manufacturing marketplace, and the reasons why a new manufacturing environment is needed. Next understand, in general terms, the tools and techniques of the three elements of MIM—TQ, JIT, and CIM. Then understand the philosophical underpinnings on which these three sets of tools and techniques are based. Finally understand how the organizational climate needs to be changed—and can be changed—in order for an environment of Modern Integrated Manufacturing to take hold.

OBJECTIVES

It is not enough any more for a manufacturing company to make money for its investors in the short term. Too often, as American and other Western companies have found through the 1970s and 1980s, decisions made for short-term financial reasons in order to heighten immediate shareholder value have worked to erode the company's long-term effectiveness as a producer of goods and services.

Those who study the few mergers and acquisitions that occur in Japan point out that when companies come together it is to enhance effectiveness in market share and research and development. The few Japanese companies that merge do so for the purpose of creating a "strategic alliance," rather than for the purpose of creating the most immediate cash value in the shortest possible time, often by carving up acquired companies.

Increasing margin and increasing market share, the two primary objectives of MIM, can only come about if products are made right, meet the requirements of customers for quality, are responsive to changes in customer desires, and are priced competitively.

To do this, costs must often be reduced. The questions are: How and where? It is best that costs be decreased by reducing waste and poor quality, thereby enhancing productivity, rather than merely by cutting manpower. For too long, companies have been trying to get rid of the most obvious cost—highly paid workers—while neglecting the more insidious costs of waste and poor quality. Too many cuts in labor have come from the parts of the manufacturing process where the labor actually adds value to the product. In addition, many of these companies have not considered the flip side of reductions in labor cost, the reduction in the amount of experience a labor force has, especially when older workers are allowed to leave through early retirement programs.

In many companies, the cost of people is small compared to the cost of materials, and even the cost of materials is dwarfed by the cost of mistakes. Walk around a plant or office and ask how much of the time is spent re-doing things because they were not done right in the first place. The answer will probably shock you. The same question can be asked about how much time spent is really adding value to a product. Ed Hay,* does a value-added analysis

---

*A JIT expert and author of *The Just-in-Time Breakthrough: Implementing the New Manufacturing Basics* (New York: Wiley, 1988).

of any plant he goes to visit before he even talks to people about instituting JIT. He finds that as little as 5 percent of activities, and less time, is often devoted to value-added steps in a process.

In addition to the possibilities Just-in-Time holds, Total Quality tools are useful to reduce the costs of not conforming to what customers want and need. An emphasis of prevention rather than after-the-fact detection eliminates large costs currently devoted to inspection. Doing things correctly the first time can also cut the costs of rework and scrap.

When labor costs are cut, the goal is often to get the biggest savings possible, and this is frequently done by trying to get older workers (who are generally at higher wage levels) to retire. There is an increasing push in the United States today to offer early retirement packages that are too attractive for most people to pass up. The result, however, is that while high direct labor costs go out the door, so does experience and, in many instances, the ability of the company to satisfy present customers and improve market share.

The final objective is to develop an organizational climate within the company that will not only allow the other goals to be met in the short term, but a climate that will *continue* to allow these goals to be met, and will allow the company and its employees to react to and respond to changes in customer needs as defined by the market.

TOOLS AND TECHNIQUES

The tools and techniques of TQ, JIT, and CIM are really quite simple. As you will see in greater detail later, the Total part of Total Quality is an organizational culture and climate issue. The Quality part of Total Quality is based on one principle and lends itself to a number of techniques.

The principle, simply put, is that quality as defined by the customer's needs and expectations must be thought about and designed and built into the product, rather than inspected for after the fact. Designing and building quality into a product starts at the beginning of the process: identifying a customer need, then designing and engineering the good or service to meet that need. It extends through every activity that has an impact on the product and ends only when the product is delivered to the customer and is accepted.

The Total Quality principle can be used to help think through ways to ensure that the product or service will do what it should for the customer. One major facet of Total Quality is finding out just what the customer expects and needs and doing so in such a way that the relationship with the customer is strengthened. Customer satisfaction and needs surveys should be used as well as top managers spending one-on-one time with customers. Another facet is a major contribution of the Total Quality movement—the concept of the internal customer. It says if you are the next person to me in the production process, the quality of your output depends on how well I do my job. If I know your needs, I should be giving you what you need, when you need it, and in the form that is most useful to you. Teamwork and the right organizational climate is necessary to support this concept and to ensure it becomes an integral and permanent part of the culture. In addition to this focus on external and internal customers, Total Quality offers tools to help make sure the product is being made in line with what the customer wants, in particular, to insure that the process is under control and does not vary unexpectedly. This is where the Quality part of Total Quality begins.

The Quality part of TQ provides two things. The first is a set of diagnostic tools, which are problem-solving techniques used to gain control over a process so that it produces a product the customer wants. These problem-solving techniques can also be used to get the process back on track if the control tools determine that something is out of control.

The second is a set of tools for maintaining control over a process. The purpose of these tools is to display clearly what is actually happening and to compare that with what ought to be happening, as the product is being designed and made or the service performed.

After the process is under control and predictable, control tools can keep the process that way in the future.

Quality begins with a product or service that is designed and engineered to meet a customer's requirements (needs and expectations). The item usually cannot also be designed and engineered to meet a designer's idea of perfection or an engineer's idea of perfection. The second consideration is to design the product for manufacturability—so that it can be made at the quality level demanded by the customer and at a cost that will not push the price of the product beyond what the customer wants to pay. Items are not usually designed and engineered for elegance, but for what the customer wants.

In the instance of services, the product is not "designed" or "engineered" per se, but the person performing the service must have the proper specifications for meeting customer demands—hotel customers want clean towels and new bars of soap, insurance customers want premium notices to be accurate and timely, and fast-food customers want their food hot and quick.

This is where the organizational culture issue plays an important role. For the Quality part of Total Quality to really work, the Total part must have begun to take hold. The Total in Total Quality becomes important when quality tools and techniques are to be implemented on a wide scale. It is then that coordination, teamwork, clarity of goals and direction, and other things that contribute to a positive organizational climate become crucial. The reality is that a Total Quality effort is a cultural change effort.

In order to have quality output everywhere, at all times, people must consistently cooperate, consider each other's needs, be focused on the same objectives, and work to the highest standards. It is the culture of a business that in many ways determines what people's attitudes are and how they will behave. If people need to alter how they are behaving in order to ensure quality output everywhere, the culture needs to change as much as anything else. Just teaching people tools and techniques is not good enough.

After this is done, maintaining quality at the source, on the manufacturing line, is really a matter of employing the tools of process analysis. First the process must be controlled, then the process must be kept under control.

First, a process flow chart is made to track the flow of the product through all its steps and stages. Next, a Pareto analysis is done to evaluate the relative importance of disturbances such as defects, machine stoppages, and late deliveries at every point of the process and set priorities for attacking those problems. The worst cases can then become the focus of more analysis or pilot programs to improve them. A fishbone or Ishikawa diagram (Figure 2–2) can be

Figure 2–2
Ishikawa or Fishbone Diagram

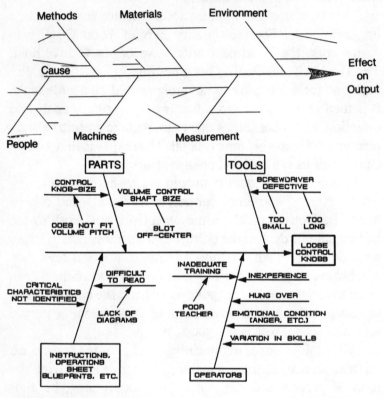

Source: Rath & Strong, Inc.

used to identify possible causes of each defect or problem. Histograms that measure what is happening and plot measurement data can help pinpoint causes of trouble. Run charts, multi-vari charts, and scatter plots offer ways to plot process data for critical characteristics to evaluate causes and relationships. (See Figure 2–3 for an example of a Multi-Vari Chart.)

Figure 2–3
Multi-Vari Chart

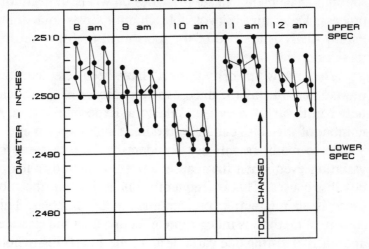

Often top management seeks to use quality improvement as the cornerstone of a major strategic effort to improve and strengthen a company's competitive edge. The results of such a strategy, properly implemented, will be increased market share and happier customers, as well as lower costs, higher productivity, and increased profits. Top management typically responds to this broader concept with considerable enthusiasm.

Although there are several acceptable ways to start, one must early on organize and implement an aggressive attack on the major causes of existing quality problems that occur in the plant and in the field.*

* Much of the material that follows on quality problem-solving tools was contributed by Tom Woods.

The first step is to identify and quantify these problems so top management can set priorities on where to begin the process. Determining avoidable Quality Costs and doing Pareto Analysis are two of the tools most useful in setting these priorities.

When a few "priority targets" have been selected, it is time to begin using the diagnostic techniques of Qualification, Multi-vari Analysis, and Factoral Experimentation. A number of variables can be tested in a single experiment.

These methods will usually identify the root cause of variation even when that cause is not on anybody's list of possible causes. This is frequently the case when the root cause is an interaction or combination of variables. This statistical method is much more effective than the classical approach of testing one variable at a time and trying to hold everything else constant. The classical method is slow and inefficient and is incapable of recognizing interactions.

Once the root causes of excess variations have been determined and the key parameters have been identified, the emphasis shifts to the various control techniques, such as Precontrol (known at General Motors as Target Area Control) (Figure 2–4), or the classical X-bar and R charts (Figure 2–5).

The key to success is to translate theory into action. Much of the actual work is performed in the plant by small cross-functional teams, assigned to attack the specific causes of quality problems in the plant or in the field.

There are also a number of techniques offered by Just-in-Time manufacturing to identify and minimize or eliminate waste and redundancy, and to maximize a smooth, one-at-a-time flow of product or services. Some of the JIT techniques are geared for manufacturing and are applicable

Figure 2–4
Precontrol Chart

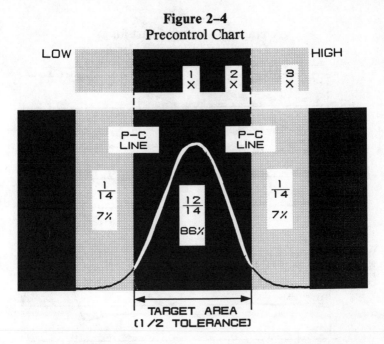

TARGET AREA
(1/2 TOLERANCE)

in any manufacturing environment. Others are applicable in all work situations.

In *work cells*, machines and workers are grouped so that a product can be moved one-at-a-time through as large a segment of the manufacturing process as possible by as few workers as possible, with limited moving, storing, and counting between manufacturing steps, and without inventory between manufacturing steps to buffer against problems of machine breakdown and the like.

Set-up reduction is a technique that permits faster changeover of equipment on the manufacturing line to shorten production runs and provide flexibility to the demands of the marketplace. The goal of JIT is for the user (in this case, a manufacturer) to produce the amount of

Figure 2–5
Average and Range Chart for
Sample Computation Process Capability

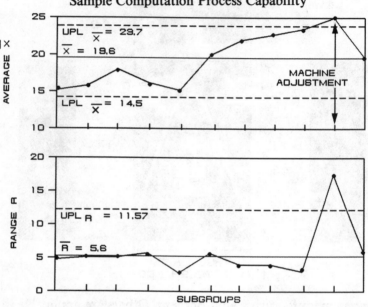

product needed for the demand each day, with no overage for inventory and no shortfall for backorders. In order to do this, production runs must be systematically cut—usually in increments of one half—and set-up time reduced proportionately. In practice, most manufacturers are satisfied manufacturing a week's worth of goods each week, rather than the more common month's worth every month or even three-months' worth every quarter.

Pull systems are used when true work cells cannot be set up or as an interim step while work cells are being designed. In a pull system, one manufacturing line signals to a subassembly line, a component provider, or a supplier, that it needs more product in order to do more work, in effect pulling the manufacturing process along.

Uniform plant load introduces two ideas into manufacturing. One is *cycle time* which states that the production rate must equal the requirement rate. The other idea is *level loading* which deals with the frequency of production. While cycle time gets the equipment running at the right speed—to meet the *need rate,* that is, sufficient products are manufactured to meet sales needs—level loading deals with producing the products with the right frequency. If every model of a product is sold every day, ideally every model of that product should be manufactured every day.

The last major JIT technique is *Just-in-Time purchasing*—determining how much purchased material is needed each day or week, finding fewer but better suppliers, and getting those suppliers to produce and deliver the amount needed in high quality goods each day or week. Just-in-Time purchasing also involves working with these suppliers to help them institute Total Quality and Just-in-Time in their own manufacturing environment.

It is important to understand that Computer Integrated Manufacturing is still making the transition from concept to reality. While computer-controlled or computer-based techniques have been employed in manufacturing for some time, the "integrated" part of CIM has remained elusive. Certainly CIM has not lived up to the claims made by its staunchest supporters several years ago.

But while integrated computer-based manufacturing is still a dream, most of the pieces of the CIM puzzle do exist, and can be used to great advantage.

There are two parts to CIM—hardware and software—

and within these two parts are a number of useful tools and techniques.

These CIM tools, techniques, and activities fall into three major categories: (1) designing the product and the process to produce it, (2) driving that process so that the product is made most cost efficiently, and (3) controlling the process so that it does what it is supposed to do. Each of these includes hardware and software dedicated to particular tasks, but the whole idea of computer-integrated manufacturing is that these separate pieces should work together harmoniously, should be able to communicate, and should play off one another smoothly.

Whether or not these elements actually become integrated is a function of how people in the company implement and commit to the integration. It is *not* a function of the hardware and software. People plan, make decisions, and set strategy; central processing units (CPUs) and data-management systems are their tools. If a leader decides that his or her organization can benefit from CIM, priority must be placed on the planning process, on building employees' commitment to change the way they operate, and on teamwork.

A major element of product and process design, the first category of CIM, is computer-aided design (CAD). CAD software stores, analyzes, and manipulates parts designs so that the design engineer can envision what the part might look like and make cosmetic changes easily, but he can also predict unusual stresses and strains on the part and alter its geometry accordingly.

While CAD software is constantly being enhanced, the basic software has existed for some time. Computers developed at a different pace, and while more and more sophisticated software was being designed, traditional

CPUs were not powerful enough to do all that engineers wanted to do. The advent of the engineering workstation, developed by Apollo Computer and now produced by a number of companies, provided a single processing unit for the most sophisticated software and offered enormous computing power to the design engineer.

Computer-aided process planning (CAPP) is that collection of software that helps plan the various steps and operations of the part. These sorts of systems generally fall into two categories.

The first category plans operations based on the operations used for similar parts previously produced. This requires a complicated library recall system, which can be very labor intensive and open to differences in interpretation and mistakes. Often, a production planner retrieves information on several parts that have characteristics similar to the part he is working on, then makes changes for the part at hand. The computer helps record and store the data.

The second category depends on algorithms that convert information on the part into lists of steps. This much more sophisticated and up-to-date technology-based option communicates electronically with the CAD system and is overseen by the production planner, whose role is less direct than in the more simple CAPP option.

Group technology overlaps with either CAPP option by offering ways to code and classify parts by similar attributes. Another element of CAPP is computerized standard data that can be used by industrial engineers to set and change work standards. The output of whatever version of CAPP is used, and its contribution, is a list of the steps that each part must go through. This is, in effect, a routing map that guides the part through the production process.

This second category of CIM consists of the tools that drive the production process in such a way as to make the product most cost efficient. It is here that the hardware part of CIM is most apparent—flexible manufacturing systems (FMS), automated assembly machines, flexible packaging equipment, robots, automated guided vehicles, and automated storage and retrieval systems. Used in the right way and at the right time, automated equipment enables the production operation to make high-quality products consistently and reduce their cost.

Just-in-Time manufacturing lays the groundwork by having grouped production equipment in cells, reduced wastes including inventory, and increased flexibility through techniques such as set-up reduction. These JIT techniques should work hand-in-hand with a total preventive maintenance system.

Controlling the process so that it does what it is supposed to do means scheduling and planning, which leads to the third category of CIM. The core of this category in many companies is materials requirements planning (MRP). MRP dates back to the late 1950s, when consultants at Rath and Strong helped to develop it.

MRP is a collection of software modules that results in valid schedules. It simulates and recalculates on a continual basis so that the production department knows more precisely what is supposed to be made, what it takes to make it, what there is in inventory, and what else is needed.

The *master schedule* says what is to be made, the *bill of material* says what it takes to make it, the *inventory record* lists what is in inventory, and the *material requirements* list indicates what must be ordered.

MRP is conceptually simple, but requires the data

storage and retrieval capacity of the computer to be used to its full potential. In the early 1980s, MRP thinking was expanded beyond the production control department, most commonly the "keepers" of the MRP system. The more MRP was implemented, the more apparent it became that the manufacturing department was operating on one set of numbers and the financial department on another. MRP II was developed to provide a unified set of numbers, using the output of MRP to generate financial numbers for a common base by which to make decisions.

When MRP was developed, JIT was not yet used in this country. MRP was designed to support a manufacturing system based on assumptions that are different from those inherent in JIT. For example, a batch orientation (not JIT) versus one-at-a-time production (JIT), and a supposition that MRP is intended to predict, give data on, and simulate inventory (not JIT) versus the elimination of inventory (JIT).

All this does not mean that parts of MRP cannot be compatible with JIT manufacturing. There is a need for scheduling and for a common set of numbers to use for planning; this is where MRP can help. At the same time under Just-in-Time, production operations are running better by simplifying, which dramatically reduces the need for many of the more complicated facets of MRP. JIT has ushered in a new way to manufacture and MRP must follow suit and be responsive to a new set of needs.

PHILOSOPHICAL UNDERPINNINGS

The three sets of tools are listed—TQ, JIT, CIM—not only because that is the order in which they should be instituted to put together a modern integrated manufacturing package, but because that is the order in which the philosophies build upon one another.

The first basic premise of the modern integrated manufacturing package is that every action has a customer, and that the goal of any action should be to satisfy that customer's needs and expectations. Too often, customers are thought of as merely the end user of a product, the "consumer." At each step along the way in any process, however, there are internal customers before the product gets to the ultimate consumer. Those customers, whether they are internal or external to the process, must be satisfied.

Simply put, if you are next to me in the manufacturing process, the quality and efficiency of your output depends on how well I do my job. In order to satisfy your needs, I must do two things: (1) I must do my job right and (2) I must give you what you need, in the form that is most helpful, when you need it. Here are some examples.

If the manufacturing line is producing keyboards for an end product such as personal computers, which will be shipped to the PC manufacturer, the ultimate customer, those keyboards must satisfy the requirements of the people in the production unit who will connect them to the central processing unit, the monitor, and the disk drives.

Similarly, if the manufacturing line is producing a machined part that will go to another manufacturing line in the same facility and be attached to other parts to become an automotive wheel brake, those parts must satisfy the internal customer's requirements first, before becoming a part of the product satisfying the ultimate customer's needs.

A different type of example would be an office processing

mortgage applications; that "line" needs to satisfy the requirements of the people who take action on whether to grant the mortgage or deny it.

Satisfying requirements is the ultimate definition of quality, not perfection, which, after all, is a subjective criterion. If the keyboard works correctly, sending the proper electrical impulses to the central processing unit when keys are pressed; if the machined part fits together with the other parts to form a brake that will stop a car; if the mortgage application has all the information necessary to make a decision; and so on, the customer's requirements have been satisfied and the Quality part of Total Quality has been accomplished.

The second major philosophical underpinning of Total Quality is "do it right the first time." The requirement for quality is not fulfilled if the customer's requirements are satisfied the second time around, after a product has been found as unsatisfactory. The keyboard should not be returned from the manufacturer to the keyboard maker; the machined part should not be sent back from the brake final assembly line; the mortgage application should not be sent back from the mortgage officer.

The Japanese first described JIT as a coherent package made up of a number of elements they had found in the 1950s and 1960s in American factories. They defined JIT as the process of using the fewest resources to produce the smallest number of goods needed in the least amount of time possible. They saw Just-in-Time as a way to eliminate waste in the manufacturing process—the second philosophical key to JIT in our pyramid.

Ed Hay "Westernized" the definition of JIT by helping to define waste in a context Americans and other Westerners understand most clearly. Hay added a new twist to JIT, the notion of "added value." He suggested that, in using JIT, that every activity carried out in the manufacturing process should "add value" to the product, and that every activity that does not add value is a waste.

Moving, waiting, unpacking, counting, inspecting, and a host of other activities do not add value, they merely add time and cost. Therefore, they are waste.

In a real way, this notion of adding value is what connects JIT to TQ, what makes a natural bridge between the two. Do it right the first time, but do it only if it adds value. There are three different kinds of nonvalue-added activities: (1) those which are the result of mistakes, (2) those which represent old habits that have not been challenged, and (3) those that are necessary because we simply do not have better ways to do something. So, while we can eliminate some, it is not realistic to eliminate all nonvalue-adding activities. But in implementing JIT as many nonvalue activities as possible should be eliminated or minimized from categories (1) and (2). It doesn't matter how good the quality is. If the activity itself comes from a mistake or old habits that should be changed, quality is meaningless. The end result should be doing the right things right the first time.

CIM adds two unique twists to our philosophical package. One is the notion of manufacturing as a total process.

The underlying premise of much of the automation or computer-aided advances that have taken place in Western manufacturing since the 1960s seems to have been to divide and conquer—take one part of the manufacturing process and automate it to the ultimate.

Most of this has happened when certain pieces of the process have broken down and someone has focused new technology on that particular problem. This has usually been done with no concern for the pieces of the process immediately before or after the problem area. The result is a patchwork quilt, something akin to a New England farmhouse that has had wings and woodsheds added over the years. There is no rhyme or reason to the architecture; the only consequence is immediate utility.

In retrospect, the New England farmhouse may be "quaint" and may "work," but the same cannot be said for information in the manufacturing company. When a piece of the process is changed under the label of "technical upgrading," its ability to interact with and coordinate with other parts of the system is generally diminished.

The irony of this is that many technically driven people move toward automation of machines or information because, as they see it, people have not been able to cooperate and integrate very well. Their response is to take advantage of the new technology and take people out of the equation. The way most high technology solutions have been thought about and implemented, though, results in machines and systems operating no better than did their human predecessors—usually worse. What makes it worse is that a leader cannot motivate a machine or do much team building with an MRP system.

Joseph Harrington said it best in his 1984 book, *Understanding the Manufacturing Process:**

What we have done is to upgrade each of the atoms of the complex without improving the total

*Harrington, Joseph, *Understanding the Manufacturing Process* (New York: M. Dekker, 1984).

structure. In spite of the crazy quilt of bandaids that cover (manufacturing), none of them cooperate . . . because they were not designed to.

One idea that CIM contributes is that it is the whole string of activities that matters, not just each discrete activity, and that it is information that connects each of these steps in the process. That information, to be useful for decision making, must be consistent and follow the logic of the manufacturing process itself.

The advent of the computer has brought both an opportunity and a problem. The opportunity is faster and more reliable information transmission and generation, and with it the ability of people to make better, faster decisions. The problem is that present manufacturing has been allowed to develop a number of "information islands," with no realization that there is a relationship and balance between them and that there is a logic that can bring those islands together. CIM offers the best opportunity to date for bringing about such a linkage.

Another major idea that CIM brings to the equation is the notion that information and analysis should be widely disseminated, rather than held by a limited number of people. Information is an asset that all involved in the manufacturing process should have so they can act on it as the situation requires.

During the heyday of MRP in the early to mid-1970s those most responsible for its development and progress concentrated on the technical aspects of their information tool, rather than the broader, organizational, people-related implications.

I have never seen an MRP system not work for technical reasons, only people-related reasons. Each time we at Rath and Strong were called in to try to fix an MRP system that had not lived up to its potential we found that the information generated, as good as it was, had not been widely shared. The information had been coveted by a few people, and the general user population had not been involved. These users did not feel a part of the process and had no sense of ownership.

These philosophical elements emphasize two overriding keys which are the essence of TQ, JIT, and CIM:

1. There should be employee involvement in decision making in the manufacturing environment.
2. Adding value must be stressed in every activity, and nonvalue-added steps kept to a minimum.

But how do we get these two things to happen? There is only one way: change the organizational climate to reward people when these elements are present rather than when they are not.

ORGANIZATIONAL CLIMATE

Our experience and empirical research at Rath and Strong indicate that there are seven major elements of the organizational climate that seem to correlate most closely with success in TQ and JIT, and that they must be adjusted and fine tuned in order for TQ, JIT, and CIM to be truly successful. They are:

1. *Influence:* People need to feel that they have influence to change things around them. JIT requires people to

change the way they do their work. But if one feels power-less to make changes over the work place and even one's individual work space, it will be very difficult to institute TQ, JIT, or CIM.

2. *Innovation:* People need to be willing and able to challenge the status quo and come up with new ways to solve problems and to do what must be done. If the climate stifles innovation, one cannot expect much progress to occur in reaching a TQ/JIT/CIM environment.

3. *Teamwork:* The ability of a group of people to work together in harmony toward achieving a commonly held set of objectives. There is a need for interdepartmental teamwork as well as intradepartmental teamwork. Much of the decision making (in TQ, JIT, and CIM) is dependent on teamwork.

4. *Satisfaction:* People need to be satisfied with their work life. Their physical and emotional needs must be met. When people are worrying about meeting mortgage payments or paying the rent, they cannot be thinking effectively about how to improve their work. If people are very negative about their work environment and feel as though they are not being well treated or not being listened to, their motivation will flag and, consequently, both innovation and teamwork will suffer.

5. *Desire to Change:* While people must have a basic feeling of satisfaction in their work life, if they are so satisfied that they become complacent, there will be no motivation to change anything. Although the most dramatic change happens when people are the least satisfied, often when an organization is in crisis this sort of change is not always the most effective and takes a significant toll on the organization. The best change comes about when

people are thinking constructively about what is good in an organization, and what can be changed to make it even better.

6. *Responsibility:* People must be willing to take responsibility to make changes. This is closely related to the issue of influence. If people feel they have influence over their work space, they are most likely to take responsibility for making the changes that should or must be made. Lack of initiative comes when a company is too paternalistic and when the company does not reward its employees for taking responsibility.

7. *A Sense of Common Vision:* People in an organization must have a sense of where the place is headed and the path that should be followed to get it there. During times of rapid change, when people are asked to alter the way they have been working, it is important that they have a mental picture of what their actions will lead to. That picture should be based on values that people can accept and to which they can relate.

Setting up these conditions so the organization can build a modern integrated manufacturing package is started during the Total part of TQ, a total team effort to bring about an atmosphere where Quality, Just-in-Time, and finally CIM can take hold and flourish.

There are some tools that can be used to adjust, change, or reinforce the correct organizational climate. These should be integrated into a strategy to manage this era and each should be used at the appropriate time. As with the Quality tools, as well as some JIT tools, they are applicable to manufacturing or service organizations and in production or administrative areas. They are:

- *Climate Analysis.* The right kind of data on the organizational climate will go a long way toward creating the sort of environment needed for TQ, JIT, and CIM. This does not mean an attitude survey, but rather the sort of survey that can pinpoint the specifics in the climate that are having the most impact on why people act the way they do.
- *Teamwork and Teambuilding Training.* I define Teamwork as the ability of a group of people to work together in harmony to accomplish common objectives. Training to bring about such a state has been available for some time, and includes ways to establish common objectives, to better understand one's own and other styles and needs, and to break down interpersonal barriers in order to allow for better communications.
- *Management Skills Training.* This includes training in such things as problem solving, decision making, creativity, and planning. It also includes training that overlaps with teambuilding, such as interpersonal skills, influence skills, and negotiating skills.
- *Reward and Measurement System Analysis.* If the reward system does not aim at the right behavior, an otherwise well-conceived TQ, JIT, and CIM strategy will always fail. Unless the measurement system operates fairly and is consistent with what people perceive to be the vision of the future, there will be disharmony, which in turn will affect other parts of the work environment. Analyzing these two systems to determine exactly what is being rewarded and measured is vital to successful modern integrated manufacturing. Any complete reward system analysis must include the

pay system as well as the promotion and feedback systems. What people get promoted, and what information is fed back and how, send very powerful messages regarding what is valued in an organization.

- *Employee Involvement Efforts.* Simply put, if employees do not feel involved in the improvement process, TQ, JIT, and CIM will not happen. These sets of tools require simultaneous actions and movement at every level of the organization.

  People will go out of their way to fix something when they have a sense of ownership in the outcome. This sense of ownership comes from being rewarded for the right actions, but more than anything else it comes from having participated meaningfully in determining the right course of action. Employee involvement efforts involve training people to act differently and develop different skills, setting up forums to provide increased interaction and joint decision making, and more and better communication between management and other employees.

COMPETITIVE VIEW

Why, if these three sets of tools and techniques seem so logical when we speak of them as a whole—MIM—are they so often seen as being in conflict?

The reason is that the organizational climate in most Western manufacturing businesses does not stress the seven elements just outlined. Most businesses stress competition rather than teamwork—divisions and departments competing for budget, manpower, and attention. Employees are not involved because they do not and/or are not allowed to participate. Reward and management systems do not encourage initiative, responsibility, and teamwork.

Some leaders reinforce the sort of climate that will undermine the effective integration of TQ, JIT, and CIM. They concentrate on the surface problems they see and the possible solutions they are given rather than taking a structured approach based on the right reasons. They do not manage for integration and unity of purpose. The typical method used in the United States is to divide responsibility and select a manager to be a champion of a particular approach. If the champion has skills to build bridges and integrate different needs and points of view, this approach makes a lot of sense, but usually the champion becomes too associated with the approach and pushes it as *the* answer.

Vice president A says the solution to the problem is automation. Okay, study it. Vice president A studies it, comes back even more enamored with automation. The company spends a lot of money on automation. It automates *what it should not be doing in the first place.* The company is still making mistakes, only faster.

Vice president B attends a JIT seminar, comes back extolling the virtues of JIT. Okay, let us see what JIT can do. Put together a JIT taskforce, JIT pilots. But it never seems to get off the ground beyond one or two pilot efforts. The taskforce, without the complete support of the top person, cannot make JIT happen because of the *necessary cultural changes that have not been made* and cannot be made by middle-level managers and shop-floor employees who feel powerless to make such changes.

Vice president C attends a workshop on Quality. That is the solution to all the company's productivity problems! He comes back and is named vice president of quality, sets up quality councils and quality improvement teams. People get excited about quality and hear its value extolled over and over again, and some quality charts start appearing tracking conformance. But quality does not improve as much as it was thought it should. The basic problem is that while there is education and a lot of talk about quality, *problems are not being solved,* and these problems are still blocking quality in the eyes of the customer.

There are two reasons these techniques when used separately will fail, or at least not succeed to the extent they should.

One is lack of a strategy that integrates the three sets of tools and techniques and institutes them in the proper sequence. The other is the lack of the right kind of leadership.

CULTURE VERSUS CLIMATE

I have touched on the issue of organizational climate in this chapter and will discuss more fully the impact of an organization's climate on TQ, JIT, and CIM in Chapter 3.

An organization's climate is a reflection of the deeper culture of a company. For a company to fully take advantage of modern integrated manufacturing, it must make changes that are deeper than the surface climatic changes— it must change the culture. Some of these cultural changes can be made before TQ, JIT, and CIM are instituted, but many more changes will be made as a consequence of the first TQ, JIT, and CIM efforts.

Changing the climate will not change the culture per se, just as putting a building full of new apartments in the middle of a slum will not change the neighborhood's character.

But making constant changes in the climate, changes that have an impact on the fabric of the culture, will inevitably change that culture, just like continually rebuilding and restoring buildings in a slum and adding some new buildings will eventually change the neighborhood's character.

David McClelland, a social scientist who spent many years at Harvard University before retiring, developed a way of assessing motivation—of individuals or organizations. He assessed motivation on three different scales—achievement, affiliation, and power.

High achievers get satisfaction from winning, competing, and doing things that are unique. Goal orientation is the key for the high achiever.

People high in affiliation get satisfaction from being close to others, being identified with a social group, a work group, or family. They may achieve a great deal by our society's standards, but it is for different reasons.

People with a high need for power get their satisfaction from controlling other people, getting others to do what they want them to.

During the Kennedy and Johnson years, McClelland used his research to predict entrepreneurial character and to try to find entrepreneurs in third-world countries who could be trained and motivated to use capitalist entrepreneurial tools to help their countries develop.

McClelland's paradigm can be used to assess companies, where they are today and where they would like to be. Then, by using certain tools, companies can be helped to change their culture so the company's reality more closely fits the dreams of its leaders.

The value of McClelland's model is that one can learn to diagnose the motives needed in particular jobs, and then measure the motives of candidates to see if there is a match. An entrepreneurial job that requires high achievement, low affiliation, and moderate power will not offer satisfaction to a person who craves affiliative relationships above all else.

Applying this paradigm to looking at organizational culture is a useful exercise as a leader begins to think about how to change the climate. If the vision calls for an entrepreneurial environment, where excellence and overcoming tough obstacles are what is needed, an organization that is highly achievement-oriented is designated. Comparing that goal to what actually exists today may show something similar to the chart in Figure 2–6, done for one of our clients.

To make such a comparison, a company must understand its culture. It can do so by gathering data on the

Figure 2–6
Chart Analyzing a Company's Organizational Culture

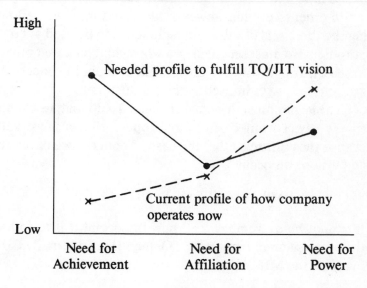

messages that are sent out to members of the company: what is written, what is spoken or acted out, and what is stressed through the reward, information, or measurement systems. Next, the company must cull from the messages the essential values relating to both the internal players (employees) and the external players (customers and suppliers).

This sort of analysis must go hand-in-hand with creating a vision of the ideal culture. Once it is clear what people would like, compare that vision to the reality and determine the steps that are necessary to bring that vision and reality together. It is here that TQ, JIT, and CIM come into play.

CONDUCTING THE CORPORATE ORCHESTRA

TQ, JIT, and CIM can be used as an integral part of getting modern manufacturing companies from their current realities to their visions, in terms of both the culture they would like to have and the technical vision they hold.

In order to do this, however, the leader must stop allowing the three sets of tools and techniques to be used at cross purposes. He must see them as a whole, and try to get others to see them that way. He must think of them in concert, as an orchestra, with himself as the conductor.

The leader must drive the changes. To do that, he cannot simply say: I want changes to happen. He must work to change the culture so that the desired congruence of reality and vision can occur.

IMPORTANCE OF PROGRESSION

It cannot be overemphasized how important it is to follow the progression of instituting TQ, then JIT, and finally CIM to create the MIM package.

Many companies ask for help in putting together a JIT environment. Often companies will have already started a TQ effort, but it will be one somewhat high on "Quality" and lacking in the "Total" aspects. In these cases, if they are thinking of launching a JIT effort, we help them take a hard look at the organizational climate and incorporate into the JIT effort ways to improve it.

We find that companies that institute JIT without first implementing TQ end up getting most of their productivity gains in the quality aspects of JIT. They may make some gains in cutting lead time, but they will often chase their tails to make some of the other gains they should under Just-in-Time. This is often because the production is not predictable. It does not have to be perfect, just predictable, and that is one of the outputs that should be expected from TQ.

In the same way, JIT cannot be totally successful without first getting started in Total Quality. TQ cannot be totally successful without thinking about following it up with JIT. If Quality is thought of without JIT, sophisticated technological inspection tools may seem like the answer to quality problems, but this is incorrect. Automated inspection may cut down the labor cost of inspectors, but it does not get to the heart of the quality issue, putting quality into the product at the source rather than inspecting for it after the fact.

If CIM is instituted without first having TQ and JIT in place, there are a number of pitfalls that can occur, including:

- Processes may be automated that should not be happening at all.
- Systems not needed will be made more sophisticated.

- People reject CIM because the right climate does not exist for its acceptance and success.
- Mistakes are still made, but made faster.

OVERLAPPING TQ, JIT, AND CIM

In an ideal world, companies would be able to take 12 to 15 years to put together a MIM package. They would be able to work for three or four years putting together a Total Quality environment before starting JIT pilot projects. Then they would be able to work for five full years instituting JIT. Finally, they would be able to assess where automation could really be helpful, given all the gains already made by TQ and JIT, and take three or four more years to institute those changes and get the systems and equipment up and running.

But today's companies do not usually have that kind of time; they are often in a fight for their very survival.

In many instances, companies will want to institute an entire MIM package in less than five years. It is difficult, but it can be done. In fact, for some it must be done. The only question is exactly how to do it. The answer for the leader is five-fold:

1. There is a logical sequence that is best for each company; find it and make sure to follow it.
2. Start with TQ, and quickly go to JIT, or start with TQ and JIT together.
3. Stress teamwork and make sure the reward system supports it.
4. Demand that there be payback early in the process.
5. Ensure that the right people are participating and feel involved.

Chapter 3

Organizational Climate and TQ, JIT, CIM

A s mentioned briefly in Chapter 2, it is important that a distinct climate be developed within the company in order for TQ, JIT, and CIM to take hold. A major portion of that climate development should take place during the first phase of a company's movement into a modern integrated manufacturing environment—the institution of Total Quality. The climate, however, will continue to be developed during the JIT phase. Although it is logical to start working on JIT after TQ has been in place for a while, it is not a prerequisite. In fact, beginning TQ and JIT together is often helpful, since it gives many technical people a better notion of what technical improvements *can be* made, thereby helping them understand the need for climate changes. It is often hard for technical people to think about climate while they are working on the technical nuts and bolts of a situation.

There are, as was said before, seven elements important to developing the proper climate for TQ, JIT, and CIM to take place. To review, they are:

- influence
- responsibility
- innovativeness
- desire to change things
- satisfaction
- teamwork
- common vision

Many people, especially those who have heard it said that the first thing necessary to bring about a JIT or TQ environment is a common vision by top management and the ability of that top management to "drive" that vision "down" through the organization, will ask why the common vision is last on the list.

The answer is simple, yet complex. The simple answer is, if the other six elements are there, the vision will be easy to create and readily embraced by the organization. The more complex answer is that when we talk first about a common vision, we are skipping the other six elements. That vision must be thought about and created by top management. The vision is something that must be caused to happen. The other six elements must exist so that people can get to the point of embracing and becoming committed to a corporate vision. A vision that is truly common will come from feelings people in the organization have, based on the realities of the corporation.

Let me try to explain why each is so important.

INFLUENCE

When I talk about influence, I mean perceived as well as real influence, the degree to which employees feel they can exercise some influence over the conditions around them. Resistance to change is higher among people who have a low sense of influence because they have no ownership in the process and less self-confidence about making changes. A low sense of influence is not limited to lower levels of the organization chart. Some top managers and many mid-level managers often feel they have less influence than they ought to have, given their relative position in a company's organizational chart. Sometimes people resist change just to exercise the influence they do have.

People with a low perception of personal influence who

are forced to participate in Just-in-Time or Total Quality efforts often acquiesce, but they usually are not energetic or persistent about the task. This may be the most destructive force in a JIT effort.

In order for TQ and JIT to be successful, people must become "empowered," that is, develop a sense of influence and control over their work environment, and a sense of confidence that they can do things for themselves. One of the things we do as consultants is study how much influence people believe they have, how much they believe others in the organization have, and how much they believe they and others ought to have. We have found that TQ and JIT work best when people have a firm "sense of place"—in the positive use of the phrase—when they believe they have more influence over changes made in the system as a whole than those below them on the organizational ladder, and less influence than those above them on the ladder. In this type of an environment, people are receptive to suggestion and vision from above, yet able to take control of that vision and make it work in their immediate sphere of influence.

RESPONSIBILITY

This means being willing and able to assume responsibility for doing things right the first time and going out of one's way to improve the environment. One who has a feeling of influence is comfortable accepting responsibility. People with a low perception of their own influence, especially relative to others, are leery of responsibility, often thinking it is merely a way for others to "dump" more work on them.

The level of responsibility is closely related to whether a

management system is in place that fosters responsibility and accountability. Companies that have grown in a compartmentalized way often have low levels of responsibility across the whole organization.

Companies with low levels of responsibility have an extra need for TQ and JIT. At the same time, it is harder to make TQ and JIT work in these companies.

In addition, higher levels of responsibility should, intuitively, correlate with higher levels of innovativeness, a desire to change, and teamwork. Those who are willing to take responsibility for actions should also be willing to take responsibility for ideas. Those who feel a sense of influence and responsibility are also willing to use those feelings to push for necessary changes. Finally, if one is comfortable taking responsibility, one should feel comfortable working with others to enhance the responsibility of a group.

INNOVATIVENESS

Innovativeness, the way it is being used here, is more of a company attribute than an individual one. The level of innovativeness in a company has an impact on people in the organization and the level of influence they feel they have.

Where do companies obtain new ideas? Are ideas encouraged from all levels of the organizational ladder? Are they listened to and considered or shot down without a thorough hearing?

People who do not feel powerful will not feel that their ideas are encouraged or taken seriously and, therefore, do not offer many ideas.

Again, people will have a perception of their own level

of innovativeness in relation to the level of others in the organization and in relation to the organization as a whole. If one feels far more innovative than those around him or her, and than the company, there could be disharmony.

In assessing innovativeness we must find out if people are allowed to be different and question the status quo, and if employees think the company's leaders want to find different ways to solve problems and will support new ideas.

DESIRE TO CHANGE THINGS

In order to implement change, there needs to be a healthy level of dissatisfaction with what exists, a desire to change things and make them better. If people are completely satisfied with what is around them, the drive to change and improve is limited.

At the same time, if the desire to change things persists without being responded to for a long time, it can turn from a healthy level of dissatisfaction into frustration. When people have crossed the fine line between dissatisfaction and frustration, the likelihood of constructive change occurring diminishes.

Many times it takes a crisis for change to occur. JIT came into being because of a crisis in manufacturing, not merely because someone thought it was a good idea.

It is not in a crisis atmosphere that the best change takes place. Once the immediate fire is put out, the real constructive change can take place. Better yet, *before* there is a fire, institute constructive change. The ideal climate in which to begin instituting TQ and JIT is one in which there is a healthy level of dissatisfaction with what exists, but not frustration.

SATISFACTION

The best change does not occur in a crisis, but *before* there is a crisis. In fact, the best change occurs when people are "basically" satisfied.

I use the word basically in a very specific way here. I mean that, in order for the best change to take place, people's basic psychological needs must have been met, as well as their basic physical and economic needs. Historians are fond of pointing out that most revolutions take place in times of relative contentment and are motivated by the middle class and working middle class, as opposed to the peasant class. It is hard to have a revolution on an empty stomach. From the American revolution to the French, from the Bolshevik to the Philippines, most revolutions occur over issues of one's rights and a struggle for power between the entrenched upper class and the working and middle classes.

As Kim Jung Ryu, a 30-year-old Korean banker, told a *New York Times* reporter in September, 1987, during strikes against the Hyundai company, "In 1960, the economy was the first problem, and the political situation was the second problem. But if a man gets food, the second step is that he thinks about spiritual satisfaction."

Among the psychological needs that should be being met in a corporate climate are individuals' needs to achieve and be recognized for achievement, to be identified with a social group and have a sense of belonging, to be challenged, to be wanted, and to be appreciated, as well as influence and confidence. Meeting these needs helps provide the motivation necessary to make employees go out of their way to improve what is around them, even if they are not specifically asked to do so.

As one of the striking Hyundai workers told *The New York Times* on September 3, 1987, "What we want is more dignity. I love my company. My basic loyalty lies with the company. But we want equal treatment. We don't want the master-servant relationship that has been traditional in Korean companies."

In addition, if people are worrying about their finances—if the mortgage or rent can be paid or where their next meal is coming from—they will not be motivated to work hard on TQ or JIT, especially if they get the feeling that TQ and JIT are being instituted as cost-cutting measures.

TEAMWORK

Teamwork does not mean that everyone is happy and that there is no conflict. It means that people trust each other and are able to work together to get the job done.

In order for people to feel comfortable in teams, they must first feel comfortable with their individual roles.

In an atmosphere where there is teamwork, issues are confronted directly, often in group meetings, and the group will stick with the issue until some resolution is reached. In many companies where decisions are made one-on-one, the resolution is often elusive because people do not buy into the decisions made.

Where there is teamwork the group participates in decision making, and in so doing group members are sensitized to each others' needs. Where there is teamwork, feelings are freely expressed, and team members' motives are open and clear. The climate continually encourages this openness.

Where there is teamwork, responsibility is distributed. People believe they are in it together; because of this help is freely offered and it is common to see subgroups spin off from the original team.

Teams share power. Credit for accomplishments is shared, and the dominant influence styles are ones based on defining a vision of the future that is common to all, and on continued participation and building of trust.

COMMON VISION

There must be a vision, created by the top person and his closest advisors, that paints an image of the future that is compelling and exciting, and around which employees at all levels can rally. This vision not only must be clear and compelling, but consistent and consistently presented in terms that are most relevant to those at each level of the organizational ladder.

It must start with agreement by top management on the values that will form the basis for the way the company will operate under TQ and JIT. TQ and JIT will not succeed if the people at the bottom or middle of the organization are operating on the basis of an idea that is dramatically different from that of the leader.

ASSESSING CLIMATE

When we go into a company for the first time to work with the leader to create the kind of climate necessary for

Figure 3–1
An Example of Climate Survey

	How often is each statement an accurate description of the situation in your organization?					How important is it that this area be improved?			
	Almost Always	More than Half	Half the Time	Less than Half	Almost Never	No Change Needed	Low Priority	High Priority	Critical

SYSTEM EFFECTIVENESS

A. Decision Making and Problem Solving

How often: 1 2 3 4 5 — How important: 1 2 3 4

1. New ideas are "shot down" before they are given a fair hearing. . . ① ② ③ ④ ⑤   ① ② ③ ④
2. People are consulted about their views before decisions are made which affect them. . . . . ① ② ③ ④ ⑤   ① ② ③ ④
3. A problem has to become a crisis before something is done about it. . . . . ① ② ③ ④ ⑤   ① ② ③ ④
4. Solutions to problems are short-sighted, resulting in more problems in the long run. . . . . ① ② ③ ④ ⑤   ① ② ③ ④
5. Decisions are avoided by pushing them up to higher levels to be resolved. . . . . ① ② ③ ④ ⑤   ① ② ③ ④

C. Information Systems

11. Reporting and measurement systems are well designed to provide information in time to correct problems before they become serious. . . . . ① ② ③ ④ ⑤   ① ② ③ ④
12. Reporting and measurement systems are well designed to help people know how well they are doing their work. . . . . ① ② ③ ④ ⑤   ① ② ③ ④
13. Performance measures around here encourage people to do things that look good in the short run, but which actually don't advance the real aims of the organization. . . . . ① ② ③ ④ ⑤   ① ② ③ ④

D. Task—Motivation

14. You get the necessary materials and equipment to do the quality of work you are expected to do. . . . . ① ② ③ ④ ⑤   ① ② ③ ④
15. Your job is challenging and leaves you feeling fulfilled. . . . . ① ② ③ ④ ⑤   ① ② ③ ④
16. Good work is recognized and appreciated around here. . . . . ① ② ③ ④ ⑤   ① ② ③ ④
17. Work is well designed and planned to get things done efficiently. . ① ② ③ ④ ⑤   ① ② ③ ④
18. People often feel bored, restricted, or controlled by the work they are assigned to do. . . . . ① ② ③ ④ ⑤   ① ② ③ ④
19. Jobs are regularly assessed to see if the work can be re-designed to make it more satisfying and productive. ① ② ③ ④ ⑤   ① ② ③ ④

20. What, if anything, should be done to change the way we make decisions, manage meetings, report information, and design work? (Limit your comments to this designated area only)

_____
_____
_____
_____
_____

DO NOT WRITE BELOW THIS LINE

	How often is each statement an accurate description of the situation in your organization?					How important is it that this area be improved?			
	Almost Always	More than Half	Half the Time	Less than Half	Almost Never	No Change Needed	Low Priority	High Priority	Critical
	1	2	3	4	5	1	2	3	4

ORGANIZATIONAL CLIMATE

H. Organizational Strategy and Communication

31. Your management does a good job laying out a plan which keeps you ahead of the field.. ① ② ③ ④ ⑤   ① ② ③ ④

32. Your management does a good job of communicating their plans to those who must implement them. .... ① ② ③ ④ ⑤   ① ② ③ ④

33. Enough time is spent to make sure everyone understands the overall operation of the organization and his/her place in it. ... ① ② ③ ④ ⑤   ① ② ③ ④

34. People at all levels have a sense of dedication to the mission or goals of the organization..................................... ① ② ③ ④ ⑤   ① ② ③ ④

I. Individual Responsibility and Risk Taking

35. Management expects you to use initiative. If you are confident you have the right approach, they expect you to act on it. ...... ① ② ③ ④ ⑤   ① ② ③ ④

36. Management trusts you to do a good job without constantly checking on you... ① ② ③ ④ ⑤   ① ② ③ ④

37. Taking appropriate risks is encouraged and rewarded.......... ① ② ③ ④ ⑤   ① ② ③ ④

38. Subordinates are encouraged and rewarded for making decisions on their own—when they have the relevant information........ ① ② ③ ④ ⑤   ① ② ③ ④

J. Rewards and Compensation

39. There is a close relationship between excellence of job performance and rewards given. .... ① ② ③ ④ ⑤   ① ② ③ ④

40. There is a promotion system that helps the best people rise to the top... ① ② ③ ④ ⑤   ① ② ③ ④

41. There is plenty of incentive for you to try to do a better job..... ① ② ③ ④ ⑤   ① ② ③ ④

42. Considering your skills and the effort you put into your work, your present salary is adequate and fair...................... ① ② ③ ④ ⑤   ① ② ③ ④

K. Creativity

43. People are encouraged and rewarded for being creative—for finding new and better ways to do things. .... ① ② ③ ④ ⑤   ① ② ③ ④

44. There is an air of excitement in this organization. People are always trying to find new, creative ways to do a better job...... ① ② ③ ④ ⑤   ① ② ③ ④

---

45. What, if anything, should be done to make sure people understand the organization's goals, assume individual responsibility to meet them in creative ways, and are rewarded for their performance. (Limit your comments to this designated area only)

_____
_____
_____
_____

DO NOT WRITE BELOW THIS LINE

Source: Rath & Strong, Inc.

the institution of TQ and JIT, one of the first things we do is conduct a climate survey that we at Rath and Strong developed in the mid-1970s. (See Figure 3–1.) This survey uses a number of questions, some of which are used in every survey and some of which are developed for the particular company being studied, to create data points that help us assess the seven elements of climate in the company. Employees at all levels of the company are surveyed and their responses can be compared with their peers, as a group against other groups, by age, gender, years of service, pay grade, and a number of other ways, all within the limits of maintaining confidentiality.

We ask employees to tell us their feelings about such things as management commitment, innovation in the company, trust, and job security. We ask their perception of how their ability to do work is affected by such things as the manufacturing process, the quality process (both technical and managerial aspects of quality), performance measurements and rewards, maintenance, their skill level, and the skill level of those they work with, communications systems, education and training programs, the work load, structures and procedures.

In the office environment, these questions are often slightly altered in wording to ask about information processing, the process by which problems are solved, maintenance of office equipment, preparation for new systems, quality of the data that they are asked to input or work with, and consistency of data with the system that has been created for them.

I will briefly touch on a few of these areas to highlight how they help us assess the seven elements.

COMMITMENT

In any change effort, the visible commitment of top management sends an important signal to the organization. Employees will ask themselves, "Is this another program that will come and go or does this require me to change if I'm going to stay on board?" and "Will this really help solve the problems that block us from doing things right the first time and adding value for the customer?"

Follow-through and persistence account for a large percent of the success in organizational change. Change takes place slowly. Success in the long run requires constant managing of the change effort and therefore the commitment of time and resources.

TRUST AND RISK TAKING

Undertaking any new endeavor requires that managers and employees at all levels be willing to risk trying new things. Risk taking requires an atmosphere of mutual trust. If employees are suspicious of each other, no one will feel free enough to take the necessary risks. This type of risk aversion is particularly true where there have been high levels of internal competition. Most modes of internal competition do not encourage trust and collaboration.

MANUFACTURING PROCESS

Predictability is a cornerstone of TQ and JIT. Reasonable control of the process is expected and documentation of the process and procedures allows for continuous improvement. The net effect of an unstable process is that it creates uncertainty and leads to redundant systems of checks and balances.

MANAGEMENT OF QUALITY

The process of solving quality problems provides a foundation for improving quality and a conduit for hearing and acting on employee suggestions. Without a process for identifying and addressing quality problems, employees become frustrated and cease to bring important issues to the surface.

Support from first-line supervisors and managers of the principles of quality sets a precedent for TQ and JIT. Management must mean business when it talks about operating under a new philosophy. Without management demonstrating commitment and modeling expected behaviors, employees see any change effort as hollow.

PROBLEM SOLVING

In order for more problems to be solved, operators need to be given more responsibility for problem solving. Supervisors need to encourage group and individual decision making and support employees in their problem-solving efforts.

For TQ and JIT to succeed, operators need to be equipped with statistical and nonstatistical problem-solving skills. Without good problem-solving skills, teams lose ground and momentum from lack of focus and ability to resolve conflict.

PERFORMANCE AND REWARDS

As a new philosophy of operating, TQ and JIT require new behaviors from everyone in the organization—increased initiative, innovation, and teamwork. Individuals must develop the habit of doing it right the first time, and adopt a willingness to broaden their scope of activities and learn new skills. The system for measuring and rewarding performance must support these new objectives and make it clear that poor performers will not be overlooked.

MAINTENANCE AND REPAIR

The maintenance department plays a central role in maintaining equipment so that quality product can be consistently produced. With high visibility and a high impact on operators throughout the plant, the maintenance and repair department can showcase customer-oriented work practices that eliminate waste. When maintenance and repair of equipment are mediocre or poor, both workers' motivation and actual ability to do quality work are adversely affected.

SKILL LEVEL

One source of resistance to change is a lack of the technical resources or skill to implement new ideas or tasks. This is particularly true in a TQ and JIT environment in which operators are expected to work across departments and specialties.

The successful implementation of the entire TQ/JIT effort largely depends on learning new skills, such as:

- Diagnostic problem solving
- Statistical problem solving
- Set-up reduction techniques
- Project management
- Statistical process control
- Teamwork.

The skill level of one's colleagues and the amount of effort they are willing to commit to getting the job done correctly can have a strong influence on one's desire to contribute and learn.

JOB SECURITY

Stability of the workforce enhances the implementation of TQ and JIT in that it ensures the presence of a skilled workforce over time. High employee concern about job security is a two-edged sword: an external threat to jobs, such as foreign competition, can stimulate working together to find creative solutions, or it may hurt employees and actually decrease motivation, because people see little hope of influencing their future.

TRAINING

If employees do not know how to do what is currently expected of them, it is unlikely they will reach the level of competence required by TQ and JIT. Every participant in TQ and JIT must know his or her role and have the skills to execute that role. In a TQ/JIT effort, team and problem-solving training, as well as supervisor leadership training, build new skills and offer a safe arena in which to model the new behaviors required.

WORK LOAD

As changes are made to improve quality, productivity, and competitiveness, it is often easier to add activities than to decide what to curtail. Coupled with cost pressures that have reduced head count, supervisors and managers may be stretched too thin to effectively implement TQ and JIT. TQ and JIT activities should be planned not as an "add on" to an individual's job, but should be staged so that they become part of the job itself.

INFLUENCE, THE CRITICAL FACTOR

While the seven elements of climate are important, and the data points help define and shape those seven elements, the really critical factor is influence. How much influence an individual feels he or she has—by itself, over work, and over leisure time—in relation to how much influence others in the organization seem to have is of great importance. Influence is a way to quantify the human side of a business, and, in effect, measure the horsepower of the organization.

Joseph Folkman, a professor at Brigham Young University, pointed out in his Ph.D. dissertation that all organizations are inherently hierarchical; if one were to graph the amount of influence people at different levels of the organization have, it would look something like Figure 3–2.

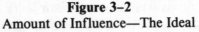

Figure 3–2
Amount of Influence—The Ideal

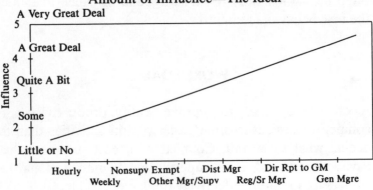

Folkman argues that the relative levels of influence (how steep the curve is) are not as important as the aggregate level of influence people have. In our society it is pretty much accepted that supervisors should have more influence than hourly workers, managers more than supervisors, vice presidents more than managers, and the general manager or executive vice president or CEO more than the vice presidents. In fact, some of our data have showed that people "lower" in an organization not only see nothing wrong with people they work "for" having more influence than they, but they feel they have more influence if they perceive the people they work for as having more influence. Although there is no "ideal" level of influence for one group or another, the goal is that the slope be gentle, so that the relative difference in influence from one organizational level to the next be somewhat constant and not too great.

When we analyze the data we rarely see a steady slope. Rather, we usually come up with something like Figure 3–3. This client is a major division of a 25-year-old company with

$2 billion in annual sales that chose to embark on a total quality effort. Since the late 1970s, the company's market had stopped growing, and there was much more competition. For the first time in its history, the company reduced its employment in 1986.

Top executives decided the company had to change the way it does business, and one way to do that was to do things better. Division officials went to the parent company to see what was possible, then called us in to guide them through the implementation process.

What the survey showed, as can be seen in Figure 3–3, is that the company was extremely hierarchical; "militaristic" was a word we heard in focus groups. As shown, the 66 percent of the division's population that is hourly, weekly, or nonsupervisory exempt, all feel they have very low influence, and there is very little slope. The slope then becomes very steep through the ranks of managers, district managers, and senior managers. We also found out that shop-floor employees and first-line supervisors found it impossible to get

Figure 3–3
Amount of Influence—The Actual Picture

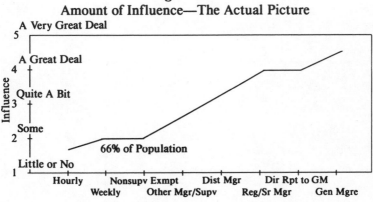

· 79 ·

decisions made; they did not believe they had the authority to take responsibility and people above them often made decisions on the basis of covering their own position rather than taking responsibility. The division is highly risk averse.

The division general manager upon hearing the feedback came away determined to improve in three areas:

- First-line supervision
- Training in problem solving, teamwork, and influence skills
- Customer service.

The goal of any attempt to change the influence pattern in a company is two-fold: to smooth out the slope so there are no major dissonances like supervisors who find themselves with no influence being squeezed out, and to "expand the areas below the curve," to increase the aggregate influence.

This can be done, and will naturally occur, as a result of a successful implementation of TQ, JIT, and CIM.

Chapter 4

Leadership Style

As was pointed out before, in order for TQ, JIT, and CIM to truly take hold in a company, the company must change the atmosphere in which people live and work, the organizational climate. If this organizational climate is to change, the company's leader must understand what that climate is now and what his vision of that climate for the future is. Then he must set the tone for the new climate if his vision is ever to be reached.

An individual leader's style has a lot to do with the success he will have in changing the organizational climate and in maintaining that change. While I have argued that for TQ, JIT, and CIM to take hold it is necessary for there to be a climate of inter- and intradepartmental cooperation, that is not to say that a leader necessarily has to change his style—to become a collegial form of leader—in order for those changes to take place. Rather, the leader must:

1. Understand the strengths and weaknesses of his own personal style.
2. Decide whether the job that must be accomplished (the creation of more teamwork and cooperation, for example) is one he is particularly good at, and if not,
3. Figure out how to ensure more cooperation and teamwork even though he does not naturally do the things necessary to bring about teamwork.

This last step may involve putting a new player in the organization who has those skills in place.

By the time most people get to the point of running an organization they have developed a style that is fairly well defined and that has helped get them to their positions. The crunch for an individual comes when the situation calls for skills other than those the person has developed.

Some people will say that the leader in those situations simply must change (that is part of the reason the management development business has become a multibillion dollar business in this country). This is what I also used to say.

But then I became a leader, and found out first-hand how hard it is to alter a leadership style. When that happened, I became a lot less glib about style change.

This is not to say that people cannot learn new management skills, and become more well-rounded people. Leaders should always strive to learn how to fill gaps in their style and become better at the art of leadership. But there is a limit to how far most of us are willing to change, or to how much time we can take to accomplish necessary changes.

Therefore, the more a leader can construct "supports" that can take care of the things he or she does not do as well as other things, the easier the task of leading will be.

To make this clear, we need to spend some time looking closely at both leadership styles and the elements of decision making and problem solving.

DECISION-MAKING/PROBLEM-SOLVING TRADEOFFS

In business, the quality of a decision is often defined as how much profit it has added to the business. A high-quality decision is one where the manager correctly weighs the profit/loss consequences in a given situation and chooses the course that is most likely to achieve profit at acceptable costs and within ethical bounds.

But whether leaders are aware of it or not, they often

stretch the elements of "high-quality decisions" to include the consideration of whether the decision to be made will have some other consequences, including:

- Satisfy or frustrate their personal values.
- Provide an outlet for expressing motives and impulses.
- Obtain approval or disapproval from people who are significant in their lives.
- Enhance or damage their self-esteem.
- Advance or set back their career prospects.
- Strengthen or weaken their political and managerial resources.

The decision-making/problem-solving process consists of four major steps:

- Identify and define the problem.
- Identify and define alternative solutions and consequences for each.
- Choose the best alternative.
- Implement the alternative.

The dilemmas of decision making and problem solving are natural, and affect everyone in a leadership position in a company. They dictate positions one takes on various topics in ways greater than most people are aware.

In addition to understanding one's personal strengths and weaknesses, it is also crucial to understand the various considerations that are present as one makes decisions to take a particular course of action.

When it comes to TQ, JIT, and CIM efforts, such trade-offs usually fall into five categories:

1. The tradeoff between what is "best" and what is realistic.
2. The tradeoff between the need for consensus and support and the need to take action.
3. The tradeoff of having staff people do a heavy screening of the vital information needed to make the decision and the possibility that such screening will distort the information and skew the decision.
4. The tradeoff between vigorous debate, even conflict, between advisors, and the tolerance of the process to function after any acrimony.
5. The tradeoff between moral and ethical ideals, and the day-to-day political realities in which decisions must be made.

One leader I know got a TQ/JIT effort going in the right way. He brought people together to hear about these two sets of tools and techniques, and managed the awareness part of the effort very well. People felt involved. He moved into the strategy phase smoothly and well, and started his top team on the road to defining a vision of how the company could be both technically and culturally.

But there the process began to bog down. He called and asked for help to figure out why. The reason was that the vice presidents felt that the leader knew exactly where he wanted to go all along, and that having meetings was largely a perfunctory step taken to follow the "right process" and have the appearance of participation. No one was willing to say it quite that way; it took quite a bit of digging to get to that conclusion. In fact, some of the team members were not aware that this was an issue until it was pointed out.

But the vice presidents were very astute. The leader really did not want his people to participate. He wanted this

TQ/JIT effort to be *his,* identified with him, and he wanted the credit.

In order to do so, he needed to push the process along and see that tangible action was taken, rather than allowing for participation by his people *and* the influence that goes along with true participation.

The considerations that tipped the scales for this leader dealing with this particular tradeoff were not "how to get the best TQ/JIT effort for the company," and not "how to do this so that it puts more money on the bottom line." Rather, the considerations on which his decision regarding the way to implement TQ/JIT were based were to satisfy his needs for affirmation, to enhance his self-esteem, and to strengthen his political standing.

When the leader was told what was going on, he did not like the message very much, and said that while the process that it was suggested his company use to implement TQ/JIT was the right one, he would make it work his way, and without help.

The last time I heard anything about this company's effort, morale was very low, there had been three different TQ/JIT coordinators in a year (it seemed no one put in the job quite measured up to the leader's expectations and the pilots never seemed to be able to get off the ground).

ETHICAL DECISIONS

This leader's choice to fake participation in the process and do things "his way" gets to the heart of the leader's challenge—to make sensible business decisions within an ethical framework.

It is one thing to know the correct answers to questions about how a company should move in a general direction, but when a leader has such a rigid idea of the direction and the answers he wants to certain questions, what the leader is really doing is manipulating people in the worst Machiavellian sense.

John Rawls, the philosopher and author of *A Theory of Justice,* argued that there are two major ideas of justice: justice as fairness, and justice as participation and relations.

It is perfectly all right for a leader to determine what is just by what is fair, in certain circumstances *and* if that leader has been properly chosen. But the whole issue of leadership begs the question about who empowers leaders, which gets to the idea of justice as participation and relations. Without participation at some level, there really is no legitimacy in a leader's actions, there really is no "his way" without others participating.

Many times, people do not sabotage efforts of leaders because they are obstreperous; they do so because they do not feel invested in those decisions, because they feel that the leader has gone beyond his legitimacy, and because he has neglected to think of justice as participation and relations.

TIME MANAGEMENT

Before getting into a detailed discussion of leadership styles, one other detail of leadership should be addressed—time management.

One role of a leader is to make decisions that set direction and policy, and to leave the details of implementation to staff people and middle management.

Regardless of how much delegating leaders do, one frequent complaint is of too little time. There are two ways to conserve time:

- Do less.
- Work smarter.

Some combination of these two conservation techniques is probably the most effective. Ways to do less include:

- Delegating, which builds subordinates' abilities, forces the leader to plan and organize, and forces objectives and authority to be clear.
- Saying "no" to "non-A" items. This keeps the monkeys on subordinates' backs.

Ways to work smarter include:

- Filtering interruptions by screening telephone calls and utilizing a secretary or administrative assistant to help set routines and protect time.
- Setting priorities: developing annual, monthly, weekly, and daily objectives, managing personal life and stress, and maintaining physical fitness.
- Developing a paper-flow system that sorts incoming mail into action, pending, and information piles, allows the leader to handle each piece of paper only once, and directs some paper immediately to others.
- Managing meeting time; for most leaders, a great deal of time is spent in meetings, much of it wasted. A well-run meeting is based on clear objectives, has an agenda, and is run in a crisp way with people who are prepared.

LEADERSHIP STYLES

Leaders with different leadership styles deal with problem-solving/decision-making tradeoffs in different ways, which will be explored as we take a look at the three basic management styles in more detail.

The Competitive Leader

The competitive leader deliberately sets up a situation where competition exists between top aides (Figure 4–1). This competition sometimes generates heat and acrimony, but it also more often than not generates the best information possible. There is often a deliberately unclear delegation of responsibilities, and the boundaries of each advisor's authority are often the battle lines, with the ultimate size of each advisor's brief being determined by conquest.

The leader is involved at all times, and the emphasis is on politically realistic or "do-able" actions.

Positive aspects of this leadership style are that it generates creative ideas, partially because of the stimulus of competition within the process and partially because the unstructured information network is open to ideas from any place. These ideas get translated into politically feasible solutions.

There are, however, a number of dangers. A competitive style places large demands on the decision-maker's time, since he is intimately involved in all of the conflict in the process. Often, the best ideas are sacrificed for the politically more feasible ones. A high level of staff competition causes both high turnover and a tendency of some staff to pursue their own interests. The inherent confusion in responsibility and authority also allows many items to simply fall through the decision-making cracks.

The competitive leader needs to be the center of decision making and has an appetite for diverse ideas, does not want to depend on any one person for input, and demands centrality and, above all, loyalty.

This is a terribly hard balancing act to maintain, because the kind of advisors attracted to working with and for such a leader are aggressive people with a relatively high need for power, achievement, and only last, affiliation. This can lead to an atmosphere with people swearing their loyalty while really positioning themselves to take over the decision-making apparatus should the leader fail or leave.

Formalistic Leader

The formalistic leader has an emphasis on order (Figures 4-2, 4-3, 4-4). Conflict is discouraged, and open expression of competition or hostility is forbidden. Issues and options are usually presented in writing. Decision making is structured, with reasoned discussions of prepared briefs. Analysis rather than implementation is stressed. The system collects data and funnels them to the top via a series of memoranda or decision papers.

Formal leaders often think that an elegant solution exists, and seek it out, putting aside considerations of political realities.

At the same time, the orderly process causes a thorough analysis of the options at a number of levels, and conserves the decision-maker's time and attention for the items of most importance.

Dangers do exist. The process is slow, and responds

Figure 4–1
The Competitive Model (FDR)

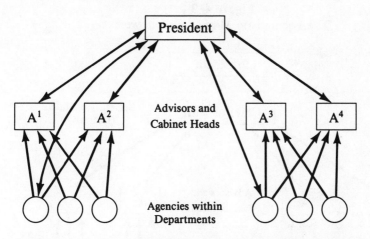

Reprinted by permission from Westview Press from *Presidential Decision-making in Foreign Policy: The Effective Use of Information and Advice,* by Alexander L. George. © Westview Press, 1980, Boulder, Colorado.

Figure 4–2
The Formalistic Model (Truman)

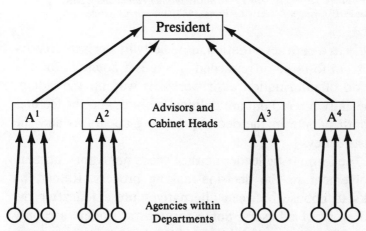

Reprinted by permission from Westview Press from *Presidential Decision-making in Foreign Policy: The Effective Use of Information and Advice,* by Alexander L. George. © Westview Press, 1980, Boulder, Colorado.

Figure 4–3
The Formalistic Model (Eisenhower)

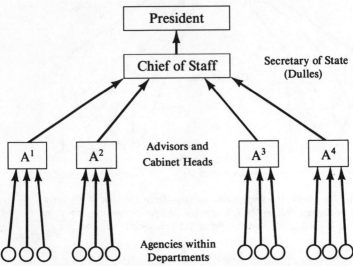

Reprinted by permission from Westview Press from *Presidential Decision-making in Foreign Policy: The Effective Use of Information and Advice,* by Alexander L. George. © Westview Press, 1980, Boulder, Colorado.

poorly in a conflict situation, especially in a crisis. Creativity is not fostered or rewarded. There is a potential for distortion of information as it works its way up the ladder. Especially filtered out are political realities and the feelings of both people in the decision-making apparatus and the constituency.

The formalistic leader neither needs nor wants intimate involvement in the decision-making process. Rather, he seeks to choose between alternatives presented after the staff work of advisors. Some formalistic leaders are only involved in steps one and three of the decision making process, defining the problem and choosing a solution. Most are

Figure 4–4
The Formalistic Model (Nixon)

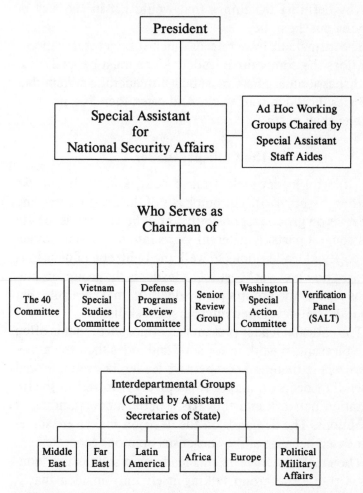

Reprinted by permission from Westview Press from *Presidential Decision-making in Foreign Policy: The Effective Use of Information and Advice,* by Alexander L. George. © Westview Press, 1980, Boulder, Colorado.

not really involved in step one; having laid out broad policy objectives they have their senior staff people define problems by defining the things that would get in the way of carrying out the policy.

The formalistic leader needs much stronger staff support than does the competitive leader. Aides must be analytical and dispassionate. There must be a bureaucratic system that produces thorough staff work. And often there is a need for a strong chief of staff.

The Collegial Leader

The collegial leader seeks first to build a team that works together (Figure 4–5). The emphasis of the decision-making process is on group responsibility, and the attempt is to fuse the strongest parts of different views into a coherent whole. The collegial leader looks to walk the tightrope of decisions that are "do-able" yet "best." The leader is the group facilitator, as well as the group's prime decision maker, a role that demands well-developed interpersonal skills.

The collegial leader presents an atmosphere that is often more pleasant to work in for staff and aides than the atmosphere where there is a competitive leader, or even a formal leader. The decision maker is positively involved in the information network and thus has a better understanding of the options. The demands on the decision maker are somewhat eased because of the consensus opinions generated.

The greatest danger in this leadership style is the "consensus trap," the group talking itself into an idea that it believes the leader is advocating. Healthy skepticism is often overshadowed by a desire not to be disloyal to the leader. The collegial leader needs to be careful to short-circuit this

Figure 4–5
The Collegial Model (JFK)

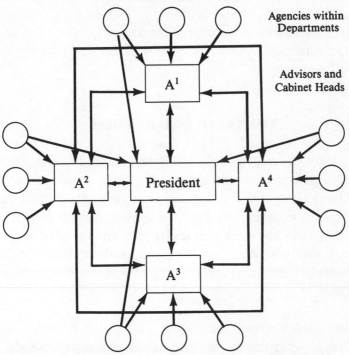

Reprinted by permission from Westview Press from *Presidential Decision-making in Foreign Policy: The Effective Use of Information and Advice,* by Alexander L. George. © Westview Press, 1980, Boulder, Colorado.

problem before it becomes acute and he loses the ability to get all of the decision options, no matter how unseemly or contentious they may be.

Other things that happen with a collegial leader are that the system places substantial time demands on the decision maker, and that it depends on people working together in spite of political pressures.

The collegial leader seeks the challenge of interaction, as well as involvement in all steps of the decision-making process.

It is necessary to have advisors who share the need for group interaction and who have the skills for participating in group consensus.

COOPERATIVE ATMOSPHERE

It does not necessarily take a collegial leader to create and foster a cooperative atmosphere. The trick is for a person who has a competitive or formalistic style to ensure that an atmosphere of teamwork and cooperation can be fostered. TQ, JIT, and CIM work best under such an atmosphere.

A leader who does not have a naturally collegial style can take a number of steps to try to foster a cooperative atmosphere.

1. Recognize the need for it.
2. Decide what has to be done to become more collegial, and take on what seems realistic to move more in that direction.
3. Determine if the people in the organization are collegial in their approach; if not, ask seriously if TQ/JIT/CIM can work in the company.
4. Look at how the top team is operating. If there are substantial barriers to teamwork, and if they are apparent to employees, do not expect the tone to be set easily for teamwork throughout the organization.
5. Look particularly at the human resources function and the director or vice president of human resources. Make

sure that the HR leader and the department are assets to creating more of a teamwork orientation in the company. This may be the most important for a formal or competitive leader.

6. Determine if members of the top team are fostering or hindering teamwork in their departments, and take action accordingly.

7. Ensure that the person charged with staff responsibility for TQ/JIT/CIM understands all this and is able to help managers build an atmosphere of cooperation, and has good teamwork skills.

8. Stay focused throughout the process, and make the appropriate considerations as he or she manages the inevitable tradeoffs.

For example, a man who had been the general manager of a $100-million company decided to retire three years hence. In that time, the company had to dramatically upgrade its operating capabilities. A strategy was defined, along with a five-year implementation plan.

The general manager had always run the company with an iron fist, making most of the decisions himself. He was wise enough to realize that it was unlikely someone else would be able to succeed who would act the same way he had.

He decided that the key element to upgrading manufacturing was teamwork, and that the next general manager had to be someone who was able to build a team. He did not have much time to find that person.

The person the general manager chose to replace him was chosen for his style, his ability to be a leader in a more team-oriented structure. That person was the human resources manager.

First, the general manager made the human resources manager the plant manager of the company's major plant, in order to gain operating experience. Then the general manager embarked on a three-part strategy:

1. Begin to implement the turnaround plan himself through improving equipment, systems, and work flow.
2. Coach the human resources manager-turned-plant manager, and shore up his lack of technical background.
3. Encourage a teamwork effort at the top level, and give it the support it needed to grow.

Even though a team-oriented style was not natural to the general manager, he fostered the change by picking a successor who had strong teamwork skills to match the task to be accomplished. The result was a successful transition, not only from one leader to another, but from one leadership style to another, one more suited to the realities of a new manufacturing business environment.

What is necessary is for the top person to develop a three-track program to get the company to the climate and technical competence he would like to see. The lowest level track runs along the technical competence. A second track runs along the climate. The highest level track runs along leadership style, and deals with the modifications the leader must make in order to make the other tracks run. Sometimes the tracks converge, other times they run parallel to each other on separate lines.

The leader manages movement forward along these tracks in three steps (which, to some extent, parallel the phases of developing a TQ, JIT, and CIM effort, which will be developed later on).

In the first step, the leader acquires an awareness of TQ, JIT, and CIM, and begins to ask what these techniques can do for this company. In the second step, the leader answers two questions:

1. Given that I believe TQ, JIT, and CIM have relevance to this company, what is my vision of what the company will look like under TQ, JIT, and CIM, both in terms of technical competence and the organization climate?
2. What do I have to do, how do I have to modify my leadership style or complement it with systems and other people in order to make that vision come true?

In the third step, the environment for change begins to be created. At the top level, the leader begins to make changes—modifications in style, new teams, new players, and new systems. On the next level are pilot programs in changing the climate, some of which will also seek to add technical competence. On the third track will be other pilot programs that are of a more purely technical nature. These may be added later, after the organizational changes have begun to take hold. (See Figure 4–6 for a schematic showing this process.)

Two situations are especially delicate, and when leadership styles clash, they tend to clash openly. One situation is when the head of a division or department within a company and the head of the entire company have different management styles. The second is when there is going to be a change in leadership and the successor has a different style from his predecessor.

When the chief executive officer and, for example, the chief operating officers have drastically different styles, how they manage their personal relations will have an impact on the atmosphere created. When a predecessor has disagreements over management style with a successor, that succession may fail.

In one situation, a large division of a Fortune 100 company was always thought of as a "snake pit," a highly charged, competitive, demanding environment. But it was no different from the rest of the company, and the company CEO was a competitive-style leader.

The newly hired division president launched a TQ/JIT effort to respond to a dramatically different competitive situation. He based the TQ/JIT effort on two simple tenets:

1. Employees must participate and feel involved in this effort, and have a true sense of ownership, in order to get results.
2. Each phase of implementation must provide a measurable return.

His boss, the CEO, saw no sense in involving employees, and offered no encouragement, but kept tracking the measures and results. As long as each phase produced an adequate return, he stayed away and the division president was able to improve the climate. In fact, the division president motivated his vice presidents by letting them know that the first time the short-term results faltered the CEO would come crashing down hard on the whole effort, jeopardizing its long-term health.

The relationship between the CEO and the division president never improved, even though there were enormous amounts of time and effort spent trying to maintain the right balance in the relationship between these two equally strong-willed and powerful people.

If that energy could have been focused on TQ and JIT, more would have been achieved faster. The fact was, though, that the dramatic difference in style required compromise and the division president did what he had to do to buy enough time to improve the climate. The CEO has since retired, and the board of directors selected the division president to succeed him. The level of teamwork this man fostered in his division went a long way toward creating the climate necessary for TQ and JIT success in the whole company.

FEEDBACK

While teamwork is a major part of the right climate for MIM, feedback is one of the pillars of teamwork. A good feedback process and an understanding of how to both present and receive feedback are key elements in making teamwork a part of an organization's climate.

Consider how one puts issues on the table, how one interacts with others when both giving and receiving feedback. The cooperative atmosphere is one in which people are communicating with each other two ways, rather than a situation where people are making information available to a leader and the leader is making the decisions. In other words, the communication is not vertical, up from staff to leader and down from leader to staff. Rather, it is horizontal, among members of a team.

In a cooperative atmosphere, feedback is constantly offered, both on substantive issues and on issues of personal style.

Figure 4-6

Graphic Portrayal of a Business Environment's Change

Tracks

	Awareness	Vision	Environment for Change
Leadership Style	What must I do to make sure we move effectively along the climate tracks?	How do I need to modify or shore up my style?	What changes must the leader make to modify style and/or shore it up with new people, systems, etc.?
Organization Climate	In what sort of climate do TQ/JIT/CIM thrive?	What will the company feel like? What will it be like to work here? How will people work together?	What pilots can begin to address climate issues?
Technical Competence	What technical competence is needed to get the most of TQ/JIT/CIM?	What will the company look like? How will work get done? How will we operate under TQ/JIT/CIM?	What pilots can begin to address technical issues?

Steps

Feedback is only useful when it is offered to help another person. The giver of feedback can maximize its effectiveness by following some simple guidelines:

- *Be descriptive, not evaluative.* Value judgments, apparent or implied, cause defensiveness and that means that the receiver is only hearing and not truly listening to the feedback.
- *Be specific, not general.* I had a boss once who gave a lot of feedback, but most was useless because he did not express clearly enough or think through what he wanted to say. The feedback needs to be put in terms that cannot be misunderstood. Most importantly, clear examples should be used to highlight points brought out in the feedback.
- *Feedback should be directed toward modifiable and relevant behavior.* Feedback on behavior that the person cannot change is frustrating rather than helpful. Feedback should also be directed toward behavior important to team goals.
- *Feedback should be well timed, offered when it will be listened to.* As soon after something happens that leads someone to want to offer feedback is the best time to give it. Feedback should be offered when there are the fewest distractions.
- *Feedback should be wanted, not imposed.* There are times when someone is just not ready to receive feedback. At such times, they will not or cannot listen. The person giving feedback can test the person's mood by asking, "Can I offer you some feedback?"
- *Feedback should take into account the receiver's needs.* Sometimes people offer feedback just to get something

"off their chest." The reason for feedback is to help someone change a behavior, not to clear the air.

A receiver of feedback also has a responsibility in the process. He or she should view feedback as a way to improve and be better able to achieve desired objectives. Guidelines for receiving feedback include:

- Be open-minded, not defensive.
- Ask questions of clarification.
- Check your understanding of the feedback.
- Make time for feedback, don't squeeze it into a period of time when there is a lot of pressure.
- Understand the needs of the person giving the feedback; it is often a stressful thing to do.

Feedback is not the only teamwork skill that is important, but it is at the core of successful teamwork. It applies to mentoring, to coaching, and to giving advice. It affects how one gets issues aired. It is vital for performance appraisal, and it is an important way to identify and diminish the interpersonal barriers that often hinder teamwork. It is an area in which the leader must hone his skills, and he must ensure that others do as well.

One way to think about teamwork in general and feedback in particular is the Johari Window (Figure 4–7). The Johari Window was developed in the 1960s by Joe Luft and Harry Ingham (hence the name, Johari) and has proven to be a helpful concept and reference for many leaders, especially those who are faced with the task of increasing teamwork.

Figure 4–7
Johari Window

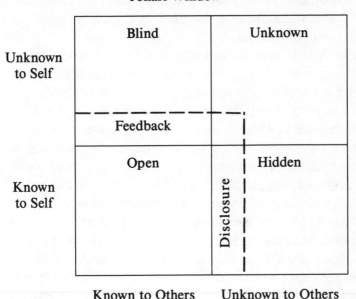

One should view the perimeters of the window as the limits of interaction with other team members. The window is then divided into four sections. The four sections are created by formulating two options along each axis of the window. On the vertical axis are the two options "things I know about myself" and "things I do not know about myself." On the horizontal axis are the two options "things the group knows about me" and "things they do not know about me."

In the "open" portion of the window both the group and the individual have a free and open exchange, when, for example, motives and rationales for positions taken by group members are clear to everyone and understandable. It is also the pane of the window where the most information is shared and when there is the most potential for trust between group members.

The "blind" area is when others pick up things about an individual of which he or she is not aware. This often has to do with nonverbal behavior and general interpersonal style, and it is here where the most opportunities for blocking teamwork exist. When others think they understand what motivates a specific person but that person is unwilling or unable to describe that motivation, there is great chance of assumptions being made about motives that turn out not to be true, and the concomitant miscommunications.

The "hidden" pane is when the individual knows the motives behind his or her behavior but others do not. The individual often deliberately keeps the motives hidden. There are times when it is necessary to do this, but if it is utilized too often in insensitive decisions, there is often a breakdown of trust.

The "unknown" area is made up of things unknown to either the individual or the group. Everyone knows that this part of the interaction exists, but it is often difficult to bring the elements that make up this hidden area to the surface.

The Johari window provides a model for understanding interaction. This model has proven of considerable help to me in consulting with leaders. Because the perimeters represent the limits of interaction, the only way to increase open interaction is to decrease one of the other three areas.

There are two categories of skills that can be helpful to increase the open area and bring about more and better teamwork, interpersonal skills, and influence skills. There are four main interpersonal skills:

- Giving feedback
- Receiving feedback
- Listening with empathy
- Communicating clearly and succinctly

There are three main influence skills:

- Exerting influence in a positive, nonthreatening way
- Confronting others effectively; getting one's own needs across without causing defensiveness
- "Win-win" negotiating; finding settlements that meet both parties' needs.

It is not the purpose of this book to delve into the specifics of these categories.

There are many training programs available for interpersonal skill development (the NTL Institute, the Menninger Foundation, and the American Management Association are a few organizations who offer them).

Influence training is harder to come by. There are many people who offer influence-training programs that are not based on good research. It is important to be sure of the credentials of any program you wish to use.

The goal of working on teamwork skills is to increase the size of the "open" square (the dotted line in Figure 4–7). This can happen if:

- A person wants to.
- The person trusts others enough to reveal perceptions and feelings.
- The leader stresses the need for doing so.
- There is enough support for the person to make that sort of change.

The leader must personally work on enlarging the open window, and must actively solicit others' help in enlarging that window. But the leader must also provide the sort of climate where others can work on enlarging their own open windows and help each other enlarge their open windows.

The role of the leader is important in ensuring that feedback is useful, and that the needs of both those giving and receiving feedback are met. The leader must let everyone know this is important by asking the right questions and challenging the managers.

Second, the leader must expect and ensure that the human resources department emphasizes feedback skills through training and development programs, and through guidelines and coaching for managers doing performance appraisals.

Third, the leader must insist that senior managers are actively giving feedback to their people and making sure they are doing the same to the employees who report directly to them.

Fourth, and most important, the leader must present a model of what is expected of others by giving feedback effectively to his own people and receiving it in a nondefensive way.

The leaders who have done the best jobs of creating teams and a collaborative climate work hard at it, constantly providing off-site training programs and practice.

The steps any particular leader must take to foster teamwork depend on his or her personal style, and should be laid out in the leader's Era Management Plan discussed in Chapter 6.

Chapter 5

Influence

A s was stated earlier, the task of leadership in changing the environment in a company is five-fold:

1. To find the logical sequence of steps and follow it.
2. To start with TQ, establish the necessary climate, then quickly go to JIT.
3. To stress teamwork and make sure the reward system supports it.
4. To demand payback early in the process.
5. To ensure that people are participating and feel involved.

In order to do this, the leader needs to exert his or her personal influence.

For the most part, when we think about influence, especially in a business context, we think about power—people who can say "do it" and have whatever it is get done. However, people are influenced to change things in many ways other than to be told to "do it."

The next few pages take a brief look at "influence styles" and explain why it is important that leaders understand and be able to display many influence styles in order to be fully effective in influencing change in their organization.

HARD VERSUS SOFT INFLUENCE

Many times a day, each person tries to get others to do something. Whether the action involved is negotiating for the sale of a house, trying to get children to behave in a certain way, or trying to get employees to think differently about the business and their role in it, people are influencing other people all the time.

The single most important skill a leader must develop in order to lead his company successfully through a TQ/JIT/CIM sequence is learning to use influence successfully. The problem is that the successful use of influence is an elusive skill for most people. The leader can use the management process discussed in Chapter 6 to sharpen influence skills in order to make the TQ/JIT/CIM process work.

The most useful model of influence has been provided by Dave Berlew, working with Roger Harrison. While there are other ways to consider this skill, Berlew's has proven the most practical and applicable.

Berlew's power and influence model was developed in the 1970s, and was in some ways the culmination of almost 20 years of work. Berlew earned his doctorate in the late 1950s at Harvard, and did his dissertation research under McClelland. After two tours as a Peace Corps country director, one in Ethiopia and one in Turkey, Berlew taught at MIT's Sloan School of Management, then started a consulting firm with McClelland. After Berlew developed the power and influence model he started another company, Situation Management Systems (SMS), to further its development and bring it to the public in the form of seminars and training programs. Berlew still runs SMS.

In his model, Berlew identified four different influence styles:

- Persuading
- Asserting
- Bridging
- Attracting

Persuading involves proposing and reasoning to influence someone. It tends to be done in a logical way and is often based on facts. People who use this style tend to do so in an assertive (but not necessarily "pushy" or overly aggressive) way. The message is "A plus B equals C, and there simply is no other option for you but to do D because all the data point that way."

Asserting is stating expectations by identifying demands, requirements, and standards. Incentives and penalties go along with this style. It is also known as the "rewards and punishments" style. The message this provides is, "Do what I want you to do and if you do you will get something you want. If you do not, you will not." Individual incentives in a factory and sales commission plans are two common examples of this type of influence.

These two styles of influence are known as "hard track." They are generally used in top-down influence, and are often the most appropriate option for some situations.

In addition, there are two other options, known as soft-track influence styles. One is called *bridging*. The leader using this style solicits different views and encourages participation. *Active listening* in the form of paraphrasing, repeating back what is heard, and asking for clarification, is a key part of bridging. The result is an atmosphere where people act a certain way because they trust each other, including the leader, and have participated in charting the path they are following.

Attracting is the other "soft-track" option; it involves a common vision influence style. Through a vision, common ground is found that highlights areas of agreement, appeals to common values, interests, and hopes. The vision is provided either by the leader or the climate.

Berlew started with some basic premises:

1. Influence is situational.
2. Influence is a skill, or several skills, that can be developed and even more easily lost—like muscle tone.
3. Those skills can be learned through training programs and practice.

I have added a corollary to these premises:

- The right influence skills exerted in the right ways will go a long way toward determining the success of a TQ/JIT effort.

People do not always get what they want. A prime reason for that is that people often use the same influence style in every situation, and some situations require different styles. The leader who is steering his organization through a TQ/JIT effort faces an enormous influence task, and the better and more facile he is at using all kinds of influence skills, the more effective the overall effort will be.

By the time we are adults, one particular influence style or another may have become "second nature," but we argue that adults can always "add to" their repertoire of influence styles. That is very important for the purpose of making change happen in a business environment.

Most leaders have risen to the top of the heap in the business world by virtue of being able to use hard influence styles very well. People have been trained to be rational and systematic, and to use facts and logic to influence others. They have been trained how to "argue the facts," which is really the persuading style of influence. In fact, hard influence styles are dominant in our culture.

However, in order to make a TQ/JIT/CIM environment really take hold, a leader will have to exert soft influence as well. The kind of cooperation and team effort that is necessary to successful implementation of TQ, JIT, and CIM can only be brought about in an atmosphere where people are employing soft influence styles in many of the situations that will be encountered.

SOFT-TRACK PATH TO MIM

The attraction, or common vision, influence style is very important in the early stages to TQ and JIT, especially when trying to get the top management team to buy into the leader's vision and the process of developing a companywide vision.

There are two ways a leader can ensure a common vision. One is by painting that vision himself. The other is by providing the forums for others to devise a vision along with him. Both ways work, and which to choose depends on the leader's skills and the situation.

To paint the vision oneself, the leader does not have to be a great and spellbinding orator. Sincerity is far more important, as is appealing to commonly held values. In fact, a leader who is too facile may come across as more smooth than sincere.

To provide the forum for others to create a common vision, the leader must be open to new ideas, and must be comfortable letting others take the lead. He must appear "influencable," although in reality he may have already planted the seeds that will lead others to "create" a vision remarkably similar to the one he would have articulated.

This requires well-honed group skills as much as it does an open mind, and must start with the leader having some basic concepts of the vision in mind.

Regardless of which way it is developed, the common vision must show a picture of the future that retains the values that are held dear. If there is an inconsistency between the values people hold as important and the vision, there will be problems.

The creation of a vision, and the influence of the leader to get people to rally around that vision, lead directly into the exercise of the other soft-track influence style, bridging, which focuses on participation and trust, In this phase, people almost "influence themselves" as they become a part of the process. They have accepted the vision, accepted that they have a say in how that vision is realized in a practical as well as a spiritual sense, and can now carry that vision forward.

The leader must be careful in his evocation of a vision to make sure that he is actually allowing for participation, and not just presenting the illusion of participation. Without true participation, there can be no real trust and without trust this influence style falls apart. People become apathetic, or openly hostile, then it is back to the need for hard-track influence styles to, in effect, ram home changes. Changes made under those conditions are not the best changes, nor are they always lasting changes.

The leader must have some flexibility regarding the vision. There must be room for the vision to breathe, to grow and expand, or be tucked in at the edges if people find it too expansive. The danger with leaders who are charismatic is that they sometimes present a vision that seems above the general populace, something out of reach that only the leader can aspire to and that, therefore, the leader must "bring to the people." In this situation, there is no participation.

If the employees respond with awe, the leader should not take this as commitment. Skepticism, questioning, with ultimate acceptance is a sign that subordinates are truly accepting a vision and assuming ownership of it, rather than responding only to the power of the leader's personality.

Without participation, there is no way for people at all levels of the organization to translate the vision into one that is meaningful to them in their working environment.

DEVELOPING HARD-TRACK AND SOFT-TRACK SKILLS

The best leaders can use all four influence styles. They pick up the cues from the situation as to what influence style will work best on the people who need to be influenced, at the time they need to be dealt with, in the circumstances under which they are operating.

But most leaders who have been well-versed and trained in hard-track leadership styles, are relatively unaware of the options open to them by using soft-track influence styles.

These skills *are not* difficult to learn. Once learned, however, they must be practiced constantly. By using a few simple techniques, leaders can better assess situations and organizations that will react to one style or another. The key is to take a systematic approach.

First, a leader must recognize that there are options to influencing people and what those options are. The leader must understand that influence is situational, and that some situations in a TQ/JIT environment may require skills that the leader has not mastered yet. He or she must understand the inevitable consequences of using one or another style. Then a leader must decide that he wants to add to his repertoire soft-track influence skills that he has not yet mastered, in such a way that they will blend in as well as possible with the more natural style.

There are a number of ways to develop influence skills, including:

- Study the great "influencers" and learn what made them that way. In order to do this, it is necessary to separate someone's political leanings from their influencing abilities. Martin Luther King, John Kennedy, Winston Churchill, Lee Iacocca, and Ronald Reagan are five people with very different political views, and very different leadership and influence styles, who have all had great success in exerting influence on people to change how they do things. There has been enough written about each of them to dissect their styles and learn from what each did.
- Just as helpful is for the leader to consider someone in his own experience whom he considers to be an effective influencer.
- Another way to develop influence skills is through good training programs.
- When a leader must develop these skills, the best way may be through imitation. The leader should find people who, for example, have good common vision and participation and trust skills, and figure out what makes them that way.

Among the set of competencies these people have are:

- The ability to describe a future state in a "tactile" way so that people can almost experience it in their mind. This is done by using words that are colorful and descriptive, and doing so enthusiastically.
- A knack for keying in on the value-based beliefs held by the people whom one would like to see change their behavior. If part of the vision of the way things will be requires teamwork, one needs to describe how in the future "teams of employees will join forces to combine the skills and insights each group contributes to solve the problems that are blocking people from being more satisfied today!"

If the leader chooses to paint the common vision picture himself, he needs to be clear about what the vision is and practice talking about it in "think of how great it would be if . . ." terms. If he chooses to form the vision with the top management team, he should have the criteria clearly in mind for the vision and spend time thinking through how to lead the group so that a collective picture emerges that fills in the detail of his basic outline.

Part of the task for the leader is to develop skills. The other part is the ethical stance, or set of beliefs he must have that will form the basis for using those skills. The leader must believe in participation. The leader must believe that people need to be involved in determining what happens that affects them. He must believe that it is important that people have visions and dreams that can be attained, and the leader must believe that it is important for everyone to share a vision of the future—a common vision so that people are aiming at the same target.

In short, the leader must work at having real compassion for the people in the organization not in a paternalistic sense of providing a house, company store, or Christmas turkey, but in the sense of providing people with the material to create a vision and with the opportunity to be players on the same team and have influence over what is around them.

Finally, a leader must develop a set of behaviors consistent with the vision he or she has helped develop.

The first time employees see the leader act inconsistently with the vision the leader is encouraging employees to buy into, the TQ/JIT effort will slip backwards. The second time it happens, progress made since the first time will be lost. The third time it happens, the damage is usually irreversible.

Communication skills are important, especially verbal one-on-one skills. The leader must be able to verbally paint a picture of the vision, not in dollars and cents but in pictures of what life will be like. He or she must speak clearly and succinctly, knowing when to stop and let others cogitate on the picture presented.

The compassion that has been developed must be translated into empathy when speaking with people. The leader must come across in such a way that people feel he or she cares and has an understanding of how they feel. The leader must listen as well as speak to people, and allow them to communicate as well as be spoken to. He or she must listen to their hopes, dreams, fears, and personal visions.

Then, the actions of the leader and organization must be

taken in harmony with the verbal message being given. If the actions do not match the words, the natural skepticism people have when it comes to changing habits will turn into frustration. Especially in the early part of a change situation, when the leader may have a much clearer idea of the vision than others in the organization, he or she must be careful not to get too far ahead. People will be tentative, and like the guide with novice mountain climbers, the leader must pause often and allow the others to catch up.

The best leaders I know are those who have learned the skills involved in all four influence styles, and more importantly know how to judge situations and determine which influence style is called for at any particular time. In short, they have mastered flexibility.

These leaders have also come to realize that in a TQ/JIT effort, soft-track styles are most critical for success because it is from them that employee commitment comes, and TQ and JIT are really total commitment efforts.

Chapter 6

Era Management

Since corporate strategic planning came into vogue in the 1960s, it has been common for people to define the life of a company as a series of planning times, each one lasting five or ten years, the standard for long-range plans.

My belief is that in all except the most conservative, static industries, once one gets beyond two or three years it is very difficult to plan, one is only drawing planning parameters. The real challenge is not to develop a plan for the next decade, rather, to develop a management strategy that is realistic for the next 18 to 36 months.

This is not to say strategic plans with a larger horizon are not valuable. Quite the contrary, they provide a long-term view, and the discipline that goes into the process has enormous value, sometimes more than the product. The point is that the strategy's time horizon is too long. To implement steps to move toward the strategic objectives, the time horizon must be shorter in order to take into account the rapid rate of change businesses experience today.

Empirical evidence has shown that every 18 to 36 months something in the internal company environment or the external business environment changes drastically enough so as to change the basis on which the long-range planning was done. Tax treatment changes. The market changes. There is a technology breakthrough. The company's leadership changes.

I call each of these 18- to 36-month periods an Era, and the development of a strategy for each era is called an Era Management Plan.

The term Era Management was coined by a friend, Alan Rush, a California-based independent consultant, in the mid 1970s. It was after the first oil crisis, and Alan and I were consulting with a company in the energy business. The company had grown tenfold in less than 10 years, from $150 million in the mid 1960s to about $1.5 billion in 1975. Customers were clamoring for their product faster than the company could make them. Everyone was looking to cash in on the oil frenzy.

The company was being run by a man with little formal training in management but with good entrepreneurial instincts who had taken over his father-in-law's company. He was good with customers, good in the marketplace, and good at motivating employees, especially salesmen. But he was used to running the company as a small business, and the task was to help him get his arms around what all of a sudden was a Fortune 200 company.

Another consultant had developed a long-range plan for our client shortly before I began working with him. That plan laid out current assumptions and major needs, and provided a strategic pathway to capitalize on what seemed to be the market opportunities at the time. It did what it was intended to do.

But that was not enough. The next step was to shape a way for this CEO to make it a reality, given his particular strengths and weaknesses and the strengths and weaknesses of the people around him. The strategy consultant he had used knew how to analyze market trends and competitive strengths, but was not expert at leadership style, organizational design, and teamwork (and did not pretend to be).

It was as though the CEO had just been given a sophisticated personal computer especially designed just for him to meet all his needs. The designers had explained the intricacies of the machine in language too technical for the CEO to understand, and the directions were not much better. He knew the machine could help him a great deal, but his background, training, and skills were not geared for the sorts of things he had to do to use it, and that made him all the more frustrated.

The primary questions we set out to answer with Era Management were:

- What is needed organizationally and behaviorally to implement the strategy?
- What manufacturing capabilities (human, physical and technical) are needed to meet the market demands forecast?
- What is required of the leader to successfully implement the strategy?
- How can we ensure the implementation strategy is flexible enough to accommodate to changes in the marketplace that were unforeseen when the strategy was developed?

Inevitably, things would happen to change the conditions under which the business operated, and that would signal the start of a new era.

What our client needed was a way to get through the one-year to three-year period, so that when the next era began he could be managing a company that was not only bigger, but better, and ready to adjust to the new realities.

This was our first Era Management test case. The first step was to understand the strategy in detail and its rationale. We toured plants, interviewed managers, conducted focus groups of employees, and met with the strategy group and people from the investment community to understand the market.

Next, the managers in the company were interviewed in

depth to assess their strengths, weaknesses, and orientation to the sorts of tasks needed to meet the company's goals.

The next step included several meetings with the CEO to decide on the time horizon for the Era Management Plan, the plan's dominant themes, the priorities (called A-items), and the specific objectives to be achieved under each A-item.

An Era Management Plan (EMP) was then drafted and reviewed, then redrafted several times. The plan suggested the events (and their sequence) that would lead to the objectives and move the organization forward in the case of each of the A-items.

Once the EMP was developed, it was time to turn attention to the CEO and the superstructure that surrounded him: the people, organizational structure, and information systems. We had to determine if the CEO's style was geared for managing the process that needed to be put in place to move forward on each A-item. We had to discover if there was balance between that style and the people, structure, and systems that surrounded the CEO. (Did the superstructure compensate for the CEO's weaknesses so that he could do what he did best?)

We found that this CEO's natural way of making decisions was to choose between options provided by others. If the options were the right ones, he almost always made the appropriate choice, because he was clear about what the broad priorities were, and they provided him clear criteria for choosing. He was not a particularly creative person, nor was he trained to deal with data and extract meaning from careful analysis.

The problem was that the superstructure did not serve him options so he could choose among them. He would receive information that was not focused for his learning style and find himself spending hours transposing it to a format better suited for him. Further, the managers around him were learning their jobs more than managing. All had grown up in the company and none had ever had a job as large as the one they now had.

Rather than having the team of advisors he needed to choose between strategic options, the CEO found himself spending much of his time reacting to problems. His style was not inappropriate for the much smaller company his used to be—one product, not a complex industry structure, the key to success being relating to customers and making sure the plant shipped what the customer needed on time.

But the energy boom had brought more and larger competition, and they were changing the rules—cost and new options for products that required high technology manufacturing equipment were now paramount.

As a result of this examination of the CEO's management style and how he functioned in the existing industry environment, we did the following:

- Devised a new information system better geared to his needs.
- Set up a new organizational structure, with fewer people reporting directly to the CEO.
- Hired a staff aide from the outside to organize data funneled to the CEO and present it to him as information he could use to make decisions.
- Created a personal development plan for the CEO to help him become a more effective leader, to hone the skills he had and develop ones he needed.

It worked. Since then, I have replicated it many times. I have found Era Management to be one of the most successful tools for corporate top managers to define the place they and their company are in, and determine how to manage the company so they are poised for the next era.

What I have also found out since the early 1980s is that Total Quality, Just-in-Time, and Computer Integrated Manufacturing are wonderful tools to use in the Era Management process.

Era Management is a quite-simple six-step process:

1. Define the time horizon of the era—usually from 18–36 months—and the two or three dominant themes of the era.
2. Create an Era Management Plan that defines the era's priorities (A-items), the objectives for each priority, the events that will produce those objectives in the appropriate sequence, and the measures needed to trace progress.
3. Analyze the leader's style, defining the leader's strengths and shortcomings, and the match between his strengths and what is needed to achieve objectives and make substantial progress on each A-item.
4. Help the leader modify his style and/or create the right conditions around him to shore up his weaknesses, in order to more successfully implement the events.
5. Begin to implement the EMP, regularly reviewing, testing, and fine tuning it in the first few months as the early events are carried out.
6. As business conditions develop and change, continue to assess the EMP and be flexible in its implementation. Events will necessitate modifications, especially after the first year. At some point (usually after 24-30 months), the conditions under which the business operates will change

dramatically, signaling a movement to another era, at which point the plan itself should be altered.

DEFINE THE ERA

The era is defined by a few central themes, each of which is supported by a group of A-items. The themes should emanate from the development of a vision for the company of where it can be at a point in the future, two or three years from the time the vision is being developed and clarified.

The themes of TQ and JIT are perfect for defining an era. For instance, three themes a manufacturing company may use to define an era are:

- Meet customers' needs.
- Reduce waste.
- Develop a teamwork atmosphere.

It is from these themes that A-items tumble out. If a major theme is customer satisfaction, a couple of A-items that come from that might be:

- Design engineers are close to the marketplace and to customers.
- Need better ways to give feedback on customer needs.

CREATE THE ERA MANAGEMENT PLAN

It is from these priorities that one can define realistic, measurable objectives, then work backwards over the era's time period and answer the question: How? After all, effective strategic thinkers plan backward rather than forward. Era Management provides a structure by which the right questions can be raised and creativity can be channeled.

From the development of themes one jumps ahead to the end of the era, a period of from 18 to 36 months, and develops A-items to move forward in that time frame. After listing what the objectives are, one can work back from the end of the era to the present, identifying the events that will lead the company to successfully meeting those objectives.

What this Era Management Plan provides is a template for the leader to overlay on a calendar, a road map of where the company wants to be, and some of the steps it will take to implement the themes and goals.

ANALYZE THE STYLE

A leader's personal style will have a large impact on how the Era Management Plan will be carried out, and whether the desired outcomes are actually achieved.

During this phase of Era Management, the leader needs to confront himself, to take a hard look at which of his behaviors might block the successful implementation of the plan. He needs to determine how those behaviors might be modified or changed, so that on the one hand the Era Management Plan has a better chance for success and, on the other hand he does not negate his style and take away his own effectiveness.

DEFINING LEADER MODIFICATION STEPS

Given the desired outcomes and the events that will have to be carried out along the way to get to those outcomes, and given the leader's personal style and its impact on the successful implementation of those events to get to the outcomes, it is necessary next to define precisely in what ways the leader will try to change or modify his style, and in what way teams or systems will be developed to complement his style.

The two major ways to complement a leader's style are with people or with structures.

Deciding the steps necessary for modification of the leader's style, then implementing leader modification steps and implementing the Era Management Plan are really one continuous process.

I have been working with companies to define eras in terms of TQ and JIT, and to develop Era Management Plans based on TQ and JIT themes, since the early 1980s, and many of those eras have recently or will in the near future come to an end. I have noticed a disturbing thing: it seems even harder for leaders to pull off the next era and implement a second Era Management Plan than it was to do it the first time.

Some companies have been at TQ and/or JIT for two or three years and now face the need to further the philosophy, extend gains, and deepen commitment. They have done alright at getting started, and for some that has meant carrying out tough decisions. But the work ahead for these companies is equally challenging. The goal of the second era, assuming that the goals of the first era have been successful, is to develop predictability and sustainability on the TQ and JIT effort.

In some ways, the easy part of Total Quality and Just-in-Time is making the changes necessary to bring them about as techniques. The hard part is making it a way of life. I will discuss this in more detail in Chapter 13, on institutionalizing changes made in the implementation process.

I am particularly concerned about the difficulty of companies to implement elements of a second era around themes of solidifying TQ and JIT gains, and making continuous improvements. The real danger is that if TQ and JIT are not made a way of life, they become another "program," the gains are not sustained, and the process is not kept under control and made predictable.

Let's speculate about some possible reasons companies are unable to consolidate TQ and JIT gains.

1. *Changes in personnel.* People leave, and new people arrive. On the one hand, the new people do not have the background of having worked from the beginning of the era and must climb the learning curve for them to get up to speed and learn the changes that come naturally to people who have been part of the effort from the start. Also, the bonds built up between managers and hourly workers when getting started in a change effort are hard to replace with new personnel.

   Second, there are internal changes. Take the example of a quality coordinator who shaped and guided a TQ effort for three years, then retired. He was so enthusiastic and committed, he did not pay any attention to developing a backup person. Many of the elements implemented were so personalized that he was just too tough an act to follow, and the TQ effort foundered when he left. Of course, the CEO should never have let this happen. The end results were a slowdown in the quality effort and lost time and missed opportunity at a time when gains should have been extended.

In another case, a director of manufacturing did such a good job at spearheading the TQ/JIT effort that he was promoted to do the same with 15 other companies owned by the same corporation. A new director of manufacturing was hired for the company, with the expectation that the TQ/JIT improvement would not miss a beat.

The result was dashed expectations all around. The person who was pulled to the corporate level found that what had worked in his division with him on the premises would not work in other divisions with him in a remote location. His style was to try something, watch people react and adjust to it, then build alliances and support—a very individualistic style that worked well as long as he was in the middle of things.

The new director of manufacturing fared slightly better. He was used to a plan, guidelines, and a strong strategy on which to base his actions. He came into a successful TQ/JIT effort that had been pieced together iteratively. He reported on a dotted-line basis to his predecessor, who did not operate that way and did not know how to provide guidelines to an effort far from his touch. The new director of manufacturing made the necessary adjustments because of his resourcefulness and persistence, but a year was wasted in the process.

2. *The company is thrown into a new era during a sensitive time in the development of the TQ and JIT effort.* If unforeseen events cause disequalibrium during a time when the TQ/JIT effort is in its formative stages, it can slow the implementation down or stop it altogether. Once the momentum has been stopped or slowed, it can be very hard to get that momentum back.

3. *The leader has backed off, pulled back his commitment.*
This can be implicit or explicit. The leader may not even
realize he has done it. He may have done it because his
short-term expectations have not been realized, or because the board of directors' short-term expectations
have not been realized and they are putting pressure on
the leader.

The role of the leader is crucial in developing and
carrying out an Era Management Plan, partially because
his style is a key ingredient in how it will be carried out
and partially because the leader sets the tone for a company's era.

A successful Era Management Plan must take into account what makes the leader tick, what he does well and what
he does not. It must ask the question *when?* When does a
leader enter the decision-making/problem-solving process?
It must also deal with the question of *what?* What does the
leader want in his life, for himself, his family, his employees,
and his business?

The goal of the Era Management process is to help the
leader shore up the superstructure around him, as well as to
develop or modify the leader's personal style. Most other
leadership consulting approaches tell the leader to change
his style, presenting a model that is often unattainable for
many leaders because it requires too much of a change or is
unrealistic given the particular situation he is in.

Era Management helps change the superstructure after
pointing out that it does indeed need to be changed. Era
Management holds up a mirror to the leader and asks: Can
your style work to help you pull off the plan needed to move
this company to the point where it must be to excel?

Chapter 7

Introduction to Six Phases

N ow that the leadership has thought about change, it is time to actually implement it. What I will formulate in the next six chapters is a six-phase process for implementing the initial change to a TQ/JIT/CIM environment.

This process should be carried out over about two years, but one should not think that when the two years are up, the task of transforming a company to a TQ/JIT/CIM environment will be complete. It will not.

The first two years are a period of "getting up to speed," of putting the pieces together so that everyone in the organization knows what TQ, JIT, and CIM are all about, and how they can help enhance the company's position and effectiveness in the marketplace.

If TQ is already in place, this process can be used to move into JIT. The process is equally applicable for situations where it will be imperative to have TQ and JIT being instituted at the same time, with pilots going on for both.

When a company gets far enough down the line in eliminating waste, deepening a climate of teamwork, problem solving, and innovation, then it is time to decide what elements of CIM make sense. At this time, everyone should have, in addition to an awareness of TQ, JIT, and CIM, a feel for the leader's vision of the company as it will be five or ten years in the future, and an idea, from firsthand work on problem-solving or explanation of the problems solved, of just exactly what TQ, JIT, and CIM can do.

By now there also should have been an identification of the issues raised by the current reward and measurement systems, and an understanding that new systems for measurement and reward will need to be applied to the work people do in the new TQ/JIT/CIM environment.

Figures 7–1 and 7–2 show this implementation process

laid out in two different ways. Figure 7–1 shows it as six separate parts. Under each part of the process are "what to do" items that outline the actions a company must take in order to successfully complete this phase of the process.

At the bottom of Figure 7–1, a third graph shows who the driving force is in each step. This line expresses my belief that only the leader can set the large policy goals, set the tone for awareness, develop a vision and strategy, and organize in a macro sense. Then he or she must hand the control over to middle management to drive the problem-solving, training, and formal education steps deeper into the body of the company's workforce. The codification of new measurement, reward, and information systems, and the deepening of a new set of company values and norms, must be driven by both the top and middle management. It is through this process of codification that the gains made by TQ, JIT, and CIM become embedded in the fabric of the company.

Figure 7–2 shows the process as a time line. In this figure, the awareness, strategy, and organization phases are finite in time, taking about six months to complete in total. The problem solving and training, education and codification are shown as continuous processes, running on parallel tracks, beginning about six months after the initial awareness phase begins, and continuing on past the end of the two-year time frame.

On the bottom of Figure 7–2 are a number of "what you get" items that lay out the benefits of each step along the way if it is done right. Figure 7–2 shows a more organic, less mechanistic, scheme for the process.

In the next six chapters, I will discuss this implementation, often in the abstract but also often with regard to a particular company, a particular "generic" or "hypothetical,"

Figure 7-1

Total Quality/Just-in-Time Implementation Approach

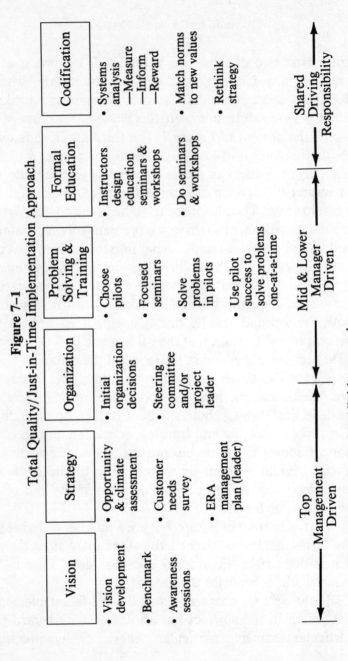

Vision	Strategy	Organization	Problem Solving & Training	Formal Education	Codification
• Vision development	• Opportunity & climate assessment	• Initial organization decisions	• Choose pilots	• Instructors design education seminars & workshops	• Systems analysis —Measure —Inform —Reward
• Benchmark	• Customer needs survey	• Steering committee and/or project leader	• Focused seminars	• Do seminars & workshops	• Match norms to new values
• Awareness sessions	• ERA management plan (leader)		• Solve problems in pilots		• Rethink strategy
			• Use pilot success to solve problems one-at-a-time		

Top Management Driven ←→ Mid & Lower Manager Driven ←→ Shared Driving Responsibility

Figure 7–2

Total Quality/Just-in-Time Implementation Approach

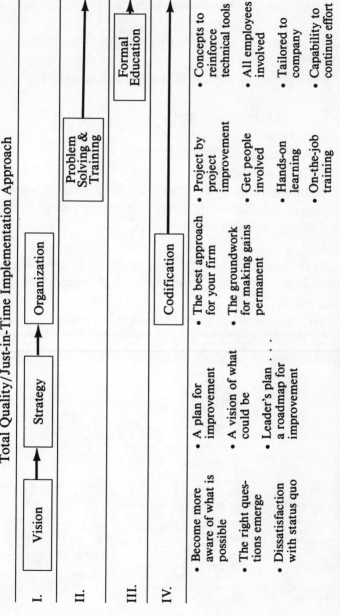

maybe even "mythical" American manufacturing company.

That company has the following characteristics:

- $500 million gross sales
- Worldwide
- Two main production facilities
- 3000 employees
- Organization: V.P. Manufacturing, Plant Manager in each production facility. The organizational chart is shown in Figure 7–3.

In the past, this company has not been known as a place where there is a lot of cross-functional, interdepartmental cooperation.

The company has been "reasonably" profitable, but has found itself recently in a much more competitive marketplace, with new offshore competition becoming evident in

Figure 7–3
Organizational Chart

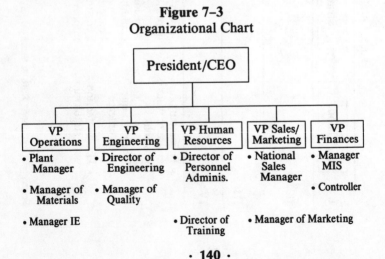

the last five years. Consequently, market share has been slipping. The company is in an industry where there is a need for more new products now than in the past, and the company has never been strong in new-product introductions.

The company has a "traditional" structure—departments of manufacturing and engineering, and a marketing and sales department that has become more aggressive in the past three or four years. The vice president of manufacturing was brought in from outside the company less than one year ago.

There is a large international union that has not been militant but is demanding more job security and guarantees. The contract is up in 18 months.

Among the particular issues are:

- The human resources group is traditional, primarily labor relations and personnel administration. The director has been there for 20 years, and came from a large steel company.
- The vice president for sales and marketing is aggressive and capable, has built a solid sales team and is starting to develop a marketing capability. He is frustrated that engineering and manufacturing have difficulty getting new products out.
- The company is relatively debt free, and has a good balance sheet. It owns property and buildings where its plants are.
- The quality shipped is among the best in the industry, but people feel it costs too much to get it; however, no formal cost-of-quality calculations are done now.
- Manufacturing costs in general are high by industry standards.

- The company often has delivery problems; not meeting commitments to ship is a regular problem.
- The company has typically taken too long to solve problems.

The President/CEO is in his early 50s, brought on board 18 months ago. He is capable, bright, and achievement oriented, but has not had a job with this level of responsibility before. He came from three larger companies, was trained in mechanical and electrical engineering, and has run manufacturing and engineering departments. His style is a combination of formal and collegial. It is a familiar profile.

It also sounds like a prescription for a company begging for the kind of changes that can be brought about by creating a TQ/JIT/CIM environment.

In order to do this, the company will have to work aggressively, yet cautiously. Let me show you how.

Chapter 8

Vision

The first element in the six-element, two-year process of kicking off a TQ/JIT/CIM effort is developing a vision of what the sets of tools can do for a company and how the philosophy embodied in the sets of tools will force the company to change. As was said before, the change should start with a Total Quality effort, then progress to JIT, and finally to CIM.

There are three parts to creating a vision: developing benchmarks for where the company should be, running awareness sessions for the management team, and finally doing formal vision development work.

If these things are done properly, within about 16 weeks the company leadership will be able to begin the second element of the effort, developing a strategy. Of course, the vision development effort will not be complete at that point, and some of the things undertaken in the vision development effort will have spawned other activities, but companies should not dally in this phase.

AWARENESS SESSIONS

Awareness sessions are meant to stretch people's horizons, to answer some questions and raise others, to raise people's commitment to change things, and to get them to begin answering the question: Why is it important to do all of this? The session, which should probably be two full days, off-site, if possible, should not be evangelical in nature, aimed at drumming up enthusiasm that may, in the end, be empty. Rather, it should be very concrete, replete with examples specifically tailored to the company, and using examples within the company. The awareness sessions must break through the understandable skepticism that a group of hard-nosed executives and managers will have about a process that will turn their understanding of business and their way of doing business upside down. The goal is to get people to think about what could be.

Although the awareness session will occur probably a month into the process, planning for the sessions should have commenced when the leader first decided to explore TQ/JIT/CIM as possible solutions. The leader should find a person to do the research and make a presentation to the executive committee. Although this person will do the initial briefing, he should not do a full awareness session, but rather should also be asked to find a consultant to conduct the awareness session and then work with the consultant in the preparation of the session. In most cases, this person should be a staff person, not a line manager. In some instances, a senior staff person, who understands how the company operates and all the nuances of both the company's culture and marketplace, is the best person. In other instances, a relatively new staff person, who is free from internal political pressure and has no vested interests, is the best person for the task. Regardless of which it is, this person should have one loyalty in this work—to the leader.

This person should be able to work fulltime on the project in order to get up to speed about TQ, JIT, and CIM before making a presentation to the executive board. A full-scale awareness session should be scheduled for a couple of weeks later.

My personal feeling is that an outsider should do the two-day awareness session. This feeling is not based solely on the fact that my firm does this kind of business.

An outsider has advantages over an insider in this kind of a setting.

1. Credibility. Outsiders have credibility in two ways. First, the awareness session will be for the most senior people in the organization, and even if the leader has full and implicit confidence in the staff person, other top management people may not. Questioning a proposal, rationale, or outlook because it comes from a person of lower rank or stature is an easy cop-out for executives and top managers to make. In addition, if there is an expense—cash being paid to a consultant—sometimes that is seen as proof that what is happening is really important.
2. More often than not, a consultant will have better presentation skills than an inside staff person, enhancing the credibility of the presentation. This is not just proposing a tactical plan; it is proposing a drastic rearrangement of how the company does business and implementing major changes over a two- to five-year period.
3. A consultant can bring perspective to the process that even the most detached insider cannot possibly have. Again, it is easy to shoot down an idea that may cause hardship if you think it is being proposed by someone with a vested interest in seeing things the way he or she is proposing to make them.

While the awareness session is planting the seeds in the minds of the management team, it should be giving the leader an opportunity to scope out how he will keep the process moving. Before the awareness session even takes place, the leader should be meeting with the consultant to help prepare the sessions and to begin talking about strategy.

Through these discussions, implementation strategy issues and questions should be forming in the leader's mind. The consultant's analysis and insights should keep raising questions about the way things are done in the company, the practices that are no longer questioned, and the norms that encourage particular sorts of behavior. It is often helpful for the consultant to do two things:

- Describe what other leaders have done when they have been in circumstances similar to those the client is currently in.
- Offer a model, a structure, through which to think about the improvement task.

DEVELOPING A VISION

The process of developing a vision will be different for each leader, depending on the leader's personal management style. Some will go into seclusion to think and create a new company in their mind; others will spend time walking around the company, collecting ideas, talking with people, and finally incorporate this information into the vision. Either way can do the job; it is all a matter of personal style.

The leader must also strike the right balance of ownership.The top team members must have as much ownership in the vision as the leader. If they do not, it will simply not become a reality. At the same time, the leader must be the driving force. How the leader manages this balance will in a large sense determine the success of the TQ/JIT effort.

The vision has two components to it—a technical component and a people component. The technical component defines what the company will look like at a certain time in the future, for example, in five years. It defines what the work processes will be like, as well as what the corporate structure and staffing structure will be. The EMP should be geared to and follow from this vision.

The people component, on the other hand, will define how the company will feel, what its values will be based on, what the relationships will be like between people within the company, between the company and its vendors, and between the company and its customers.

However the vision is developed, it must relate to the marketplace. The vision of the company in the future must be in terms of how the company will react to the changing marketplace, how it will increase market share and compete more effectively. The vision cannot be one simply of cost reduction, belt tightening, and elimination of labor through automation. Without realistically assessing and monitoring the changes in the market, the company might lose its reason for existing if it focuses too much on nonmotivating factors such as cost cutting.

A vision based primarily on dramatically reduced costs runs the risk of conveying that cost cutting is *the* way of making things better. Aiming at a future state of lower costs and having to get there by cutting the head count and squeezing in other areas is inherently demotivating for most people.

Cutting costs may be a necessary step to rectifying past sins and setting things right, but it is only a step in the direction of something better, a better way of manufacturing life.

A vision needs time to percolate through the top management team before the organization is ready to embark on the problem-solving, education, and codification processes.

Once the leader has put the vision into a relatively coherent form, he or she should begin to talk it over with some of the key people in the organization, the people who have influence.

This should start with the leader asking questions, questions that elicit responses that tell him if key players have a vision similar to his; or, if they do not, letting him assess whether instilling his vision in these people will be easy or even possible. In other words, the leader should be testing the answers to his questions, but not expecting certain answers or penalizing people for not giving certain answers.

As the leader plants these seeds of his own vision with the key players by asking questions, he should be using the responses to those questions to formulate a plan of how he will work to get that vision firmly implanted in those key players, so they can pass it to the rest of the members of the organization.

At the same time, the leader must be open to being influenced. Part of achieving ownership of the vision by the top team involves the leader engaging in some "give-and-take," and letting other people put their brand on the vision rather than simply embrace the leader's vision.

One way to do this is for the leader and the top management team to attend a vision development workshop, again working with the consultant who led them through the awareness session.

When incorporating TQ, JIT, and CIM into a vision of the company in the future, it is important to remember that these are ways to get somewhere else, not an end in and of itself.

The vision clarification process will probably go through a sequence such as this:

1. The leader becomes dissatisfied with the way things are in the company. He is frustrated by losing market share and the problems that are not getting or staying solved. He begins to search for a way to make things better, and learns of TQ and JIT. As part of this, the leader must be close to his customers and understand their frustrations and needs. It is not yet time for a formal survey, but it is time to get some information.

   The danger, of course, is increased polarization as some of the people may feel defensive about the president going directly to customers. The upside is that questions are becoming further clarified for the leader:

   - Why can't we solve that quality problem permanently?
   - What does that competitor know that we do not?
   - Why don't my people spend time coordinating instead of defending turf?

   The realization hits that: If that is the way the market is going, the way we have always operated just will not be good enough in the future.

2. The leader charters an awareness session with his top team, and likes what he hears. The simplicity of TQ/JIT is appealing, and the completeness of the philosophy helps him crystallize the questions he needs to ask to get at the root causes of his dissatisfaction and frustration. Often here there are skeptics on the top team as well as supporters, polarization occurs, and the leader must assume the delicate task of encouraging discussion to get

ideas and issues on the table without implying which he thinks is best.

3. The leader starts looking, with the aid of benchmarking, at what other companies have done. He should be interacting with other leaders in those companies to find out what their companies do well and why.

If the leader does all this work alone, he runs the risk of making the vision so personalized that others will not have a chance to make it theirs. This can exacerbate whatever polarization already exists.

The ideal is that throughout the process, the leader is asking questions of his top people to make them think.

4. The leader looks at his own values and at what he wants for the company and the employees.

5. By the time he gets to a vision development workshop, the leader should have formulated key questions and already done some preparation. The consultant should be the spearhead of this process, helping the leader think through the issues, format the questions, and help set up the benchmarking visits and customer needs survey.

The vision development workshop should answer these questions:

- What are the basic underlying beliefs about how to run this business, the principles on which the ideal company should be built?
- Given what we now know, if we could wave a wand, where would we be in X years (depending on the industry, people usually think in terms of two, five, or ten years)?
- What is our de facto vision? If nothing changed, where

will we be in X years? Given what we are doing now, where will we be then?

- What are the differences between these visions? What are the underlying philosophical elements of each, are they the same, somewhat different, or dramatically different?
- How do the answers to the first two questions square with what our customers said they want?
- What are the forces that currently exist that can move us from where we are to the picture formed by the answer to the first question? What are the hindering forces? (These forces can be thought of as technical, physical, climate, and people forces.) What is the rank order of changing them, and how difficult will it be to change them?

As a result of the vision development workshop there should be movement in the direction of the vision that is built on TQ and JIT principles. People should end the workshop feeling as though they have moved forward and have crystallized questions that have yet to be answered. It should clarify the positions of the people on the top team regarding the future of the business.

As the vision is formulated, it will be increasingly important to "compare" it with the existing strategy. If there is a strategy that was created based on the current set of assumptions, it must be determined if that strategy is compatible with the answer to question one, or will it have to be adapted once the vision gets crystallized.

Throughout this process, the leader must make sure the steps move forward, and he must keep asking questions and listening very hard to find out what people believe, where they stand, and how they will behave. If the vision development workshop does what it is supposed to do, the groundwork will be laid for the final steps.

6. The output of the vision development workshop needs to be tested, thought through, and debated by the top team and others the leader asks to join the process, and the basic concepts and values must be tested and made concrete.
7. When the leader thinks the time is right there should be a "vision development workshop II" to paint a clearer picture of the vision. This more well-defined vision will continually be tested as the TQ/JIT implementation process progresses.

BENCHMARKING

At the same time as the vision development process is taking place, the company can begin the process of "benchmarking." Benchmarking in this context means determining the areas of production and service where the company needs to improve, then finding the companies that are the best in that area of business. The companies studied do not have to be in the same industry in order to learn about the process under study.

For example, Xerox determined that it had to shore up its distribution system. What company did it turn to to learn about distribution? L.L. Bean.

The companies could not be in more diverse businesses—Xerox in high technology and L.L. Bean in clothing and sporting goods. The two companies' individual distribution systems could not be more different—Xerox through sales representatives and dealers, L.L. Bean through catalogues and one store that caters to tourists in Maine. Despite these differences, Xerox learned a lot about distribution from Bean.

People get intrigued with benchmarking and identifying what other companies do very well and why. For this reason, benchmarking is best done by a taskforce made up of the "best and brightest" from a variety of departments. Because much of this work is both creative and independent, it is important to have people who are inquisitive, dogged about getting information, and able to dig deeply and ferret out why something is so good. This is not the time to take people who cannot do this job well and give them a learning experience.

FOOLS JUMP IN
(WHERE CONSULTANTS FEAR TO TREAD)

In a multidivision or multiunit company, one division or unit should become the test case for the change to a TQ/JIT/CIM environment. The danger of an awareness session is that everyone comes out of it so hyped up they all want to get on with the program. In this case, the leader must help decide which division to begin with.

One project we were involved with that was not successful occurred a couple of years ago when the chairman of a large company decided that a massive quality effort was the key to increasing market share and making his company more prosperous. We were hired as the consulting firm to help with the change. We spent about four weeks gathering information about the company and preparing an awareness session for the top team, including the corporate leadership and the general managers of all 13 divisions that would eventually be involved.

At the end of the second day, we sent the general managers home for the night and told them to think about whether they wanted to be the pilot program division. The next morning they all came back and said, yes. This was the beginning of December. We suggested that there really should be only one pilot division, that everyone take a few weeks to think about it, and that we would iron it all out after the Christmas and New Year holidays.

On Christmas Eve, the person coordinating the project for the chairman called and said everyone was convinced to go with all 13 divisions at once. They wanted to run awareness sessions that would be mixed, both in terms of divisions and level of management. We again tried to convince the company that they should go one division at a time, that awareness needed to be tailored to a particular division and that they really needed to assess the progress of one pilot before jumping in to the other 12 divisions. We should have said: No!

Because the company wanted awareness sessions for hundreds of people by March 1, we left it to the client to conduct orientations. What we ended up with were hybrid awareness sessions: people who were from manufacturing with people who wanted to use it in nonmanufacturing areas, people from three or four different levels of management, people whose production systems were nothing alike, and people who had varying amounts of orientation before attending the sessions.

It was a mess. It is also important to point out that the TQ/JIT effort weathered these initial problems and has gone on to be very successful. We all learned something from this incident.

The point of all this is that TQ/JIT is not just another program, and cannot be dealt with the way one would deal with an MRP installation.

Because we are talking about the basis on which one does one's job, it needs to go gradually, iteratively. We are not talking about just filling gaps in knowledge, but also about changing attitudes, behavior, and skills. It is best to get a "natural work group" (a boss and his direct reports) together and grapple with these issues, exploring and discussing, not just listening to outsiders make presentations. Another lesson learned is not to go too fast. By opening the gates and exposing people several levels down into the organization to some new ways of thinking, the process got somewhat out of control.

As I have said before, the process must be allowed to "percolate" through the organization, and the leader must keep his finger on the pulse of the organization to make sure the time is right for the institution of each part of the process.

THE LEADER'S TASKS

The major task of the leader in the vision phase is to ensure there emerges a vision to which top management is committed. This does not mean that top management merely understand the leader's vision; that requires no true commitment. Being committed means feeling deeply about the vision and being spurred on to do what it takes to make it a reality, especially something that is uncomfortable like changing established, comfortable behavior patterns.

There are two ways the leader can approach this task. He can think hard about the vision and get it to the point where it can be described and then talk about it every chance he gets. The other way is to provide forums where the vision emerges from several people as a result of an intense discussion. In the former, the leader is more active, more in the center of the vision, and there is more of a danger that others will go along but not be truly committed (remember the "consensus trap"). Either of these approaches can be successful, though, and selection depends on the leader's personal strengths and preferences, and the type of people around him. When in a rebuilding mode when top management staff may change, the leader may choose to be more direct. But let me be clear about one very important point that is central to my advice on vision development. Either option must be done in a way that lets people influence the leader. Otherwise there will be no ownership in the vision, and without ownership there can be no commitment. If the leader is comfortable with Option 2 (a function of his style and the quality of people around him), he must manage the process by asking questions and by drawing out and helping to clarify what is on the minds of other employees. Patience along with questioning and listening skills will bring results. If Option 1 is more appropriate, the leader must convey to the top management group that he can be and *wants* to be influenced.

Throughout this process the leader must focus his attention on the top management group. Once he is convinced of the commitment of these people, his attention must turn to insuring that they do the same with their people as he has done with them. Commitment cannot be forced or legislated. It grows as the process trickles down through the organization. The end result should be a central vision of what the organization could be that (a) is owned by each employee and (b) each employee interprets individually as a personal vision of what he/she wants to accomplish through work life. The leader can provide the glue to bring these separate interpretations into a single mosaic by supplying and reinforcing a few central themes, then backing off and letting people define their vision of life in the future organization around those themes.

There is one other aspect about common vision leadership that is important to mention. The best process to create a common vision is the one that works smoothly and naturally . . . where there are no major glitches and where the top managers participate equally, each providing a part of the direction of the process. This does not just happen. It is the result of flawless thinking and preparation of the leader that go into setting up this sort of vision clarification process. But it is often not apparent that the process has been carefully thought through just because it seems to go so smoothly and naturally. With a society like ours which makes so much of solving problems, the people who make certain that problems don't happen in the first place do not get much credit. This is especially true with vision development. The leader who gets credit or adoration will have his ego satisfied temporarily by people who will tell him what he wants to hear, but will not end up with widespread commitment to a common vision. The objective for the leader must be a *common* vision, not to get credit for being the author of one.

A last note on this topic, the role of those around the leader. Just as there are tasks facing the leader, there is also a great deal of responsibility that falls to other employees, the responsibility of followership. Many leaders have strong personalities—they are determined, tough people who are used to getting things done. They have been rewarded for their achievement-orientation or perhaps took the hill themselves. Sometimes they can be intimidating, even when they don't want to be. Such leaders certainly have to convey they can be influenced and then show flexibility; that is their part of the relationship. But intimidation is something requiring two people. There must be a person who feels intimidated for every person who acts in an intimidating way. I often encounter people who don't practice good followership because they refuse to or do not know how to confront someone with a strong personality. They don't say what is really on their minds, don't voice concerns, and don't challenge when they should. Many, though, are quick to be critical in private, or worse after something goes wrong. The point I'm trying to make to employees other than leaders is to think hard about your part of the responsibility for making MIM a success and don't leave it totally to the leader.

Chapter 9

Strategy

As soon as possible after the awareness session is held, the leader must begin to formulate a strategy for the company which determines how the tools of TQ, JIT, and CIM will be used. Strategy is really a vision of what the company should be at some point in the future and a plan for how to get there.

This is the part of the process that the leader must really get excited about, because only the leader can spearhead a coherent strategy and have the political and formal power to pull the organization to make his vision a reality.

The creation of a strategy really entails three stages; an opportunity and climate assessment to test the realities of the company against that vision, a complete customer needs survey, and the creation of an era management plan for the leader to help him guide the firm through the period during which the corporate vision will, it is hoped, come to life.

This process of strategy creation should take between two and three months, and could be going on concurrently with more indepth benchmarking. At the end of the strategy-creation process, the company will be able to set up an organization for carrying out the process and begin to solve problems, set up formal education for the entire company, and codify the changes into a new set of rules, regulations, systems, and corporate values.

OPPORTUNITY AND CLIMATE ASSESSMENT

The awareness session and benchmarking should have presented a basic picture of opportunities. While in phase one, it was adequate for the leader to talk to people and get anecdotal evidence about the corporate climate. In this phase, a more formal vehicle is necessary to determine the opportunities and climate with more precision. The best vehicle for that is an opportunity and climate assessment, a survey that answers the questions:

- What are the specific, realistic, and measurable opportunities available through TQ and JIT?
- Is the company's organizational climate supportive of the needed changes?

It also helps answer the question:

- Is the company ready technically to make the change?

The assessment pinpoints where opportunities are for improvement in the company. The list below is indicative of typical opportunities, given in terms of percentage reduction or increase our clients have achieved:

- Lead time: 89–92 percent reduction
- Direct labor productivity: 20–50 percent increase
- Indirect labor productivity: 20–60 percent increase
- Scrap and rework: 25–65 percent decrease
- Price of purchased materials: 10–50 percent decrease
- Inventory including
  —raw materials: 35–75 percent decrease
  —work in process: 70–90 percent decrease
  —finished goods: 60–90 percent decrease
- Set-up time: 75–95 percent decrease
- Space needed: 40–80 percent decrease
- Capacity: 35–50 percent increase

It allows the company to set dollar or percentage goals for improvement, and sets a baseline with which to judge progress and measure improvements in these areas.

The assessment also identifies what people/cultural barriers exist in the company that will have to be lessened or overcome in order to achieve the opportunities and make TQ/JIT/CIM a reality, and what people/cultural facilitating factors there are in the company that should not be diminished in any way.

By pinpointing technical opportunities and identifying cultural factors that can either help or hinder the process, the assessment provides a basis for specific implementation plans that can be developed. One way it does so is by identifying potential pilots, as well as the systems and attitudes that will need to be changed and codified throughout the process.

The opportunity and climate assessment (OCA) helps the process of getting involved in the TQ/JIT effort. Upper and middle managers should participate along with those conducting the assessment to uncover the possibilities.

A byproduct of the assessment that is not so apparent is that it increases employees' general awareness, an important prerequisite to learning that will take place in the formal education later on. The assessment also increases commitment to the effort by involving a broader employee base early on. As the entire process of creating a TQ/JIT/CIM environment is carried out, these less visible benefits can, in some instances, turn out to be more important than the hard information that is gathered through the process. (See Figure 3–1, pages 70–71.)

The opportunity and climate assessment is a good time

to get the company's human resources department heavily involved in the process. Of course, the vice president of human resources should be one of the people in the leadership group that has gone through awareness and vision development work. That person should be asked to bring in some other human resources personnel to assist with the opportunity and climate assessment, and contribute to the people/cultural portion of the assessment. By being involved now these people will be prepared when they are asked in subsequent phases to put together formal education programs and proposals for new reward systems from the results of the OCA.

A small taskforce, made up of people from inside the company and one or two from the consulting organization, should develop and carry out the survey. This group should include people from different organization levels as well as different departments.

The OCA should be done through interviews with individuals and focus groups, questionnaires, analysis of written data, and observation. Whether Rath & Strong's methods are used, or someone else's, some general guidelines include:

1. People should be oriented thoroughly regarding the purpose of the OCA, what will be expected of them, what will take place, and what will happen to the data.
2. The data must be fed back to the people who gave it. Data feedback may not seem like the most important thing to the OCA team or the leader, but it is critical to the people who offer the data.
3. OCA results must be balanced by providing both:

- quantitative, measurable opportunities and climate issues to be addressed and
- positives and negatives.

4. There must be a solid analytical model at the core of any OCA. The outside consultant who walks through the shop and then gives a list of ten things that are wrong is not only unprofessional, his comments simply will not be accepted. There must be an analytical model that provides a solid, defensible rationale for conclusions.

5. The OCA team should recommend the next steps to fix the climate issues and to achieve the opportunities identified. This plan should be realistic, specific, and measurable.

6. As much as possible there should be commitment to the plan from the people who will have to carry out the changes. That commitment should develop from their involvement in the OCA itself. A measure of such commitment is whether the client personnel who are to be involved in implementation help feed back to top management the results of the OCA along with the consultant. Some of the most effective implementations we have been involved with are ones where just this has happened. Because people have put themselves on the line to top managers, they have more ownership of results and more commitment to solve problems.

CUSTOMER SATISFACTION

In the early stages of all efforts to change the way a company operates, three questions must be asked:

- What do customers want and need?

- Can we deliver products or services now that meet those needs?
- How better can we meet those needs?

Leaders who have a background in marketing or sales have developed their own systems over the years for judging customer needs. Many of the best leaders spend four or six hours per week visiting or on the telephone talking to their customers and old contacts.

But many corporate leaders have not risen in a company through the sales and marketing departments, and are not attuned to customers. Therefore, leaders who are trained as lawyers, financial managers, engineers, or in some other way, may need a more formal mechanism for gauging customer needs and satisfaction.

I recommend spending about six weeks gathering data about TQ/JIT/CIM and how it is having or could have an effect on the company in the marketplace. These data will help in the development of awareness sessions. This data-gathering activity should be done by the person assigned by the leader to spearhead the effort, along with the outside consultant who will conduct the formal awareness sessions.

At the same time, the leader and the person to whom he has assigned this task should work to develop a formal customer satisfaction survey. Another six weeks or so should be taken to conduct this survey with key customers and a cross section of other customers.

The survey should be a written document, but should be followed up by phone calls to selected customers, preferably from the leader. The leader should ensure that his top team and selected others do the same. This helps share the load and, more important, it gives the vice presidents first-hand experience listening to the customers. Four hours in total per day on the telephone talking to customers is not too much for the team to spend during this period.

The kinds of questions that might go into a survey are:

- Are we responding fast enough to your changing needs?
- If you could change three things about the way we do business, what would they be?
- Comment on our quality.
- Rank us versus the competition.
- What are your general needs today? What will they be in the next 18–36 months? What can we do in that time frame to get more of your business?

The results of this survey should help the leader and his advisors sit back and say: In order to achieve X, the company needs to do Y.

This will be a vital piece of information for the leader to have in order to launch into the creation of a strategy as soon as the rest of his management team has become aware of the plans and visions.

ERA MANAGEMENT PLAN

About mid-way through conducting the OCA survey, the leader should begin the process of mapping out the next corporate era. The Era Management Plan process will continue beyond the time when the OCA is fed back, but the OCA will provide some useful information for the Era Management Plan and it is appropriate to begin at this point. The

OCA process usually takes six to eight weeks. Once it is done and feedback has been provided, the leader will be ready to begin the process of defining an era and finishing the Era Management Plan.

The OCA should lead to a more definite vision of what could be and to some definite targets for the administrative departments and plants for the next five years. It should also indicate to the leader the elements that can be forged together to shape themes and A-items.

There are really two separate plans. One is a plan for achieving the specific opportunities identified in the OCA, while the Era Management Plan should offer a way for the leader to steer the organization in the appropriate way to create a TQ/JIT environment. While the two clearly must overlap and complement each other, one is aimed at specific, measurable targets while the other (the EMP) is a personalized plan tailored to the particular style of the leader to move his company to a point where people can achieve such opportunities on a continuous and ever improving basis.

Chapter 10

Organization

Once a general level of awareness has been reached among the top management and a strategy has been developed for putting in place the tools of TQ, JIT, and CIM, it is time to put together the organizational structure under which these changes can begin to take place. If all has been going well, this organization should be put in place after about six months in the process of developing the TQ/JIT/CIM environment, and should last for about 12 to 18 months more, although sometimes it will be necessary to keep the organization in existence longer. The organization should be evaluated every six months starting after one full year.

This organizational "phase" itself should not take a long time to implement. If the proper groundwork has been laid by the awareness sessions, the benchmarking, the vision development, and the creation of the strategy, putting together the right organization to manage the improvement process becomes almost instinctive—the right person to be project leader or coordinator will almost invariably become identified by this time and the organizational decisions will often seem the natural thing to do as they are made in an informed way.

Companies that we have seen that have had problems in conducting pilots and problem solving had trouble developing organizations. Things were not thought out clearly, and not enough time was spent in the decision-making process of this phase. Poor groundwork led to the wrong people being chosen to head up the effort, given the particular situation.

One big question is: Should the process be managed by a team in the form of a steering committee, a project leader, or both?

In most instances, the answer is both. Since teamwork is one of the attributes that is stressed in the new environment, it clearly makes sense to establish a team to bring that environment about. A project manager is not always necessary, but often is. For the sake of our discussion we will assume the need for a project manager.

There is always the need for someone to spearhead a change effort like this. The question of how much individual effort it will take has a variety of answers; there is a continuum from a full-time project leader to project champions who are senior managers with many other responsibilities. The answer to how much of someone's time is necessary depends on two variables:

- *The people involved.* Are they able to spend the time needed? Are they used to taking on responsibilities in addition to their regular jobs?

  One client gives senior managers responsibilities for projects such as delivery problems and customer satisfaction that cross the whole corporation, in addition to their normal responsibilities. The JIT effort in this company was championed by the general manager of one of the largest divisions for almost three years. Over this time, he maintained his regular duties while being the corporate-wide JIT champion, although he learned to work smarter in his own job and had to delegate more responsibility to his subordinates—they of course were all in favor of their boss continuing his ad hoc role indefinitely.
- *The culture.* The culture must be one where there is more cooperation than competition between units, for a senior manager to make something like this work. If

the culture is highly compartmentalized, like that of our hypothetical company, the stage will not be set for success. In our hypothetical example, there would likely be a need for a separate project leader because of the internal competition and compartmentalization that exist. A senior manager or subgroup of the senior staff, or even one department taking on the task, would not be likely to succeed.

PROJECT ADMINISTRATION

From many companies we have seen, the most obvious temptation in picking a project leader, and the temptation to avoid most assiduously, is to pick a "good old boy," someone for whom there is abiding corporate loyalty but who is not currently doing a very good job where he or she is. This is often an older worker, one who is finding it difficult to make the changes necessary for the company to make. This is exactly the wrong person to choose, since the project leader is, in a real way, a partner of the leader and the top team, and together with them is responsible for pushing those changes down into the fabric of the organization.

Although it will be necessary for managers and divisional executives to carry the message to their people, the project leader is responsible for coordinating and making sure everyone has the same information at the same time, and for troubleshooting and solving problems within the process itself.

The project leader must be flexible and able to work in a constantly changing environment. It is imperative that the project leader be someone who is not tied to the old way of doing business and does not have a vested interest in seeing that one particular group within the corporate organization gains primacy over other groups or over the process.

This person must also be willing to stay in the position for as long as it takes to get the job done (probably 12 to 24 months) but not one minute longer. He or she should not be using the position of project leader as a stepping stone to a higher management position, and should not try to make the position a permanent one with a staff, budget, and constantly increased funding.

This person's loyalty should be only to the leader, not to other individuals in the company. But the person should get along with other members of the top management team and should have easy access to these people who have their own constituencies within the corporation. These "influencers" or "stakeholders" are the people who will ultimately take the message to their constituents—the employees in their departments or divisions.

Here is what one client did that worked well. The company had just completed a major reorganization and cost-reduction process, and the leader did not want to pull anyone out of an already pulled-tight top staff. The leader was able to persuade a man who had just retired after a very successful career to come back as a consultant. The man had no ax to grind against anyone in the organization. He had been well liked and respected. He constantly pushed away opportunities to "collect a department" under him. What he really wanted to do was finish the job and return to the gentleman's farm he had bought.

Finding this person reinforced the fact that the project leader's job is temporary. The introduction of TQ and JIT went very smoothly and after 12 months, he went back to retirement, and the line managers assumed responsibility for implementation.

The decision to have a full-time project leader has these considerations: Pro: (1) it is usually faster because he or she can devote more time to the task, (2) it offers centralized responsibility so that the leader has one person to look to. Con: (1) there is a danger that just one person will make things happen . . . this has led to personality cults or just plain overdependence. If it is decided to appoint a full-time project leader, there are some things to keep in mind. Figure 10–1 shows the characteristics that seem to make the difference between average and excellent TQ/JIT program leadership. When it is decided that having a full-time project leader is the way to proceed, candidates should be matched with these 22 items.

Figure 10–1
Twenty-two Competencies of a TQ/JIT
Project Administrator

1. Able to implement without taking credit
2. Able to organize work and bring about order from chaos
3. Able to effectively set priorities
4. Able to keep priorities clearly in mind
5. Knows when to push and when to wait
6. Gains satisfaction more from goal attainment than from teamwork
7. Gains satisfaction from knowing things he is responsible for are under control
8. Thrives on predictability, and structures things he is responsible for so they are predictable
9. Able to traverse organizational boundaries smoothly and equally effective in different organizational settings

---

10. Has influence skills developed to the point where he can be equally effective with different senior managers whose styles vary widely
11. Able to listen actively so that the other person feels comfortable sharing information
12. Able to figure out how to structure an effort so that people from many different camps feel involved
13. Has loyalty to the leader and to his vision of how the TQ/JIT effort should be structured
14. Is much more attuned to short-term goals than to a more nebulous, long-term vision
15. Cares more about getting things started than about carrying them forward for a long time, and is happy to pass off responsibilities as long as the goals he has set out to achieve are attained
16. Works in a deliberate way and makes steady progress, even if some see him as plodding
17. Works iteratively, in a building block fashion
18. Automatically breaks a long-term task into shorter-term steps that are more easily envisioned
19. Does not care about building a staff, having a title, or creating a power group
20. Buys into the TQ/JIT philosophy and believes deeply in its precepts, but is not dogmatic
21. Is more solid and dependable than flashy and exciting
22. Is more practical than ideologically pure. Searches for ways to negotiate and move around obstacles and is satisfied with having gotten 80 percent of what is needed instead of stubbornly holding out on ideological grounds and perhaps getting nothing.

STEERING COMMITTEE

While it is not always necessary to have a separate, full-time project leader, the formation of a steering committee is imperative to bring about the change to a TQ/JIT/CIM environment. The way the group works will also be important to success. The process simply will not work unless a sense of teamwork and collaboration is developed.

The people on the steering committee need to be department heads. In our hypothetical company, which has little tradition of working together, that is even more important than it would be in a company that has had a tradition of teamwork.

One part of the steering committee's process of getting organized will be formal teambuilding sessions, again probably led by an outsider. Even without these formal sessions, their group should have gone through several TQ/JIT-related experiences together by now—such as benchmarking visits and awareness sessions. From these events, the team should be at the point of having the shared experience of getting to know what TQ and JIT are all about. They should also understand each others' positions and biases.

The leader must push the message that teamwork is a prerequisite for making the necessary changes occur. The leader must identify the project leader, put together the steering committee, and run the steering committee aggressively and visibly for the first 12–18 months. The project leader should act as staff to both the leader and the steering committee. This is a delicate role.

Eventually, the leader should turn over the reins of the steering committee to someone else if he decides the steering committee will continue to play a valuable role. A senior manager who will lead vigorously and with imagination, and who buys in deeply to the TQ/JIT philosophy is the right person to take over at this point. It may be a younger manager whom the leader wishes to test in a situation such as this. It may also be a more seasoned manager whose "even hand" will guide the steering committee into another phase.

Either way, the project leader's role remains a crucial one, and he must strike the balance between loyalty to the leader and loyalty to the new steering committee head. This can become very delicate since the project leader has become a source of information to the leader.

This transition should not be made until:

1. The initial goals are achieved.
2. The group is working effectively as a team.
3. The leader is convinced that each member of the steering committee is committed to TQ/JIT success.

The leader, as he backs away, may find a small void created with regard to the changes and the excitement necessary to bring the changes about, especially if he is a charismatic leader. The steering committee, working under a new leader, gradually fills that void, creating a solid base of support for the changes that can then be filtered into the various departments and divisions of the corporation and communicated to every individual.

As the void becomes apparent, it is vital that the leader not jump back into the breach, believing that he was leaving too soon and he now must return to save the day. One of the precepts of TQ/JIT is pushing real decision-making authority down to lower levels in the organization. If the leader cannot allow the transition of authority to the steering committee to take place, it is doubtful that people will believe he can do it elsewhere.

At this point, as the process is moving into the pilot phase, the leader's role splits. On the one hand, he or she must stay involved with the steering committee, but really only peripherally and as a catalyst, a prodder and a counselor, especially to the new committee chairperson. The new chairperson must have the day-to-day organizational control as the process moves into pilots, so team members do not think they need do nothing unless the corporate leader is there urging them on. The leader's second role at this point is to begin thinking long range again, especially about what systems are going to have to change to make TQ, JIT, and CIM permanent fixtures once they catch hold. The leader should be thinking in terms of measurements, rewards, and information systems, and how and when the new systems will be codified, and how to move the process into other parts of the company.

The leader should constantly be on the lookout for signs that the steering committee has outlived its usefulness. After an initial 6- or 12-month honeymoon, there should be formal reviews every 6 months to make sure that it is still necessary and that it is doing the job it was supposed to.

The steering committee is not a standing committee, but an ad hoc structure separate from line management. The committee should not be entrenched. If the steering committee has too much power, or is seen as having too much power, the process of change can be hurt. The process of forming a TQ/JIT/CIM environment is really up to the line organization, and there must be a feeling of "ownership" of

TQ, JIT, and CIM by that organization. A sign that the steering committee has become too strong is: It is not important for the line manager to get involved because the steering committee runs it.

There are a few signs that the steering committee is getting into trouble. One is when decisions that should be made in the normal course of day-to-day business, or in the company's management committee, are put off until the meeting of the steering committee (which often includes some of the same people as the management committee).

The second is when the steering committee begins to look for more ways to stay in existence. One tip-off to this is when the initial goals are being met and everything is proceeding on target, yet the steering committee begins to set goals that require it to continue in control rather than passing responsibility for the effort to the line managers.

The steering committee cannot take the place of managers and management decisions.

Steering Committee Charter

When the steering committee is formed, a "charter" should be defined. The charter is, in effect, a document that grants it the right to exist, lays out its rights, its responsibilities, and its relationships to other parts of the organization.

The charter needs to define who the people are that will serve on the steering committee, the goals of the committee, the anticipated duration of the committee, and the procedure for reviewing the committee's work. Committee members' work on the committee should be included in their performance reviews.

A model charter may state that:

- The purpose of the TQ/JIT steering committee is to launch the operational excellence effort effectively. The steering committee will exist for as long as it takes to do so, and not one day longer.
- It will be made up of the leader and his direct reports, plus the project leader. In addition, others may be added as the steering committee thinks appropriate.
- The steering committee will meet once every two weeks for the first six weeks and once a month thereafter. The mode of operation will be teamwork, with open discussions at all times, direct confrontation of barriers to the group's working as a team, and frequent feedback to and from team members.

The steering committee's initial goals are:

- For second-level managers to become aware of TQ and JIT principles
- To ensure their commitment to the effort
- To assess the opportunities and climate in order to select and launch pilot programs and monitor their implementation
- To ensure that what is learned is documented and used in subsequent programs.

In addition, the steering committee will be a policy-making body for the effort, setting direction and establishing the basis on which it will proceed. This will be based on and will follow the principles already defined for the operational excellence effort. It will report to the management committee for the duration of its existence.

Chapter 11

Problem Solving

Once the organization is established, the company can begin doing selective problem solving. This process, which continues for at least the next 18 months (until the end of the two-year break-in period), accomplishes a number of goals. Some of the goals are specific, helping to change one particular aspect of the system, while others are more general, establishing a tone for the TQ/JIT/CIM environment.

Tackling problems one at a time, using a team approach, gets people involved, provides hand-on learning and on-the-job training, and provides the opportunity to closely measure improvements as they occur on a project-by-project basis.

The first few problems tackled are test cases or pilots. The knowledge and ability gained from completing these pilots will make it easier to complete the next pilot; and once pilots have been completed in a number of different areas, the knowledge and ability gained help to solve specific problems as they are dealt with.

The steering committee must stay on top of things and see that resources are allocated so that no systemic barriers get in the way of progress. The steering committee must run interference for the pilot, anticipating what barriers there are within the corporate structure that will interfere with or conflict with carrying out the pilot—such as productivity measurements, overtime, work rules, or reward systems—and how they can be overcome.

The project leader must work as a coordinator, or liaison, between the steering committee and line management, presenting line management with a single voice. He or she should not be seen as being an overseer, however, since line management must always be in control of the individual pilot process.

CHOOSING PILOTS

Ideas for pilots should come from the opportunity and climate assessment (OCA) survey, where employees and consultants flag areas that need change and prioritize them.

When a pilot is chosen, the line management work with the project leader and the people from the human resources department to put together focused seminars that enrich or build the skills necessary to carry out the pilot.

The steering committee figures out how many pilots to run, which pilots to run, and when to run them. Pilots should be run in areas other than manufacturing. Examples of nonmanufacturing gains to be made from TQ and JIT will help people in office departments believe these tools apply to them.

It is helpful for a company to start with one pilot project in one plant, and a second pilot in the corporate staff system. As one pilot runs its course, another should start immediately. Too much time lag between projects allows enthusiasm to wane. Too much time doing "post mortems" on past projects also allows people to find and dwell on the mistakes, not the gains. Mistakes made should be flagged, but only so that they can be corrected quickly—one of the tenets of TQ.

Pilots should not go on longer than necessary. Once a moderate skill level has been developed, the gains of these pilots should be turned on increasingly difficult problems. In a year or 18 months, the committee can report that X projects—20 to 30 is not unreasonable—have been completed, with Y results—percentage gains or reductions in certain areas. It is very important that pilots early in the process should produce short-term, tangible results.

Pilots chosen should be challenging yet realistic. They should not be problems that have proved intransigent in the past. There are three goals of a pilot:

- To solve a real problem where the solution will make a difference, not a problem that does not count.
- To show drastic results in a short time using new techniques (this will spur interest).
- To learn techniques that can be replicated to solve other problems.

Reducing order-entry errors is a good example of a TQ pilot opportunity. Diagnosing what actually happens; determining if the process is in control; if it is not, why it is not; and finding ways to improve the process are some of the tasks the pilot can take on.

Set-up reduction is a good JIT pilot to work with. Companies have regularly achieved at least 75 percent reduction in set-up time, often within six weeks, using the right techniques.

PEOPLE AND PILOTS

It is important to get the right people involved in pilots. The "right" people include:

- Stakeholders, people with real and perceived power, who have constituencies (i.e., certain leaders in middle management supervision and the labor force).

If these people understand the power of the pilots, they will surely influence others who will follow their lead.

- People who will talk to their peers about the pilots. Their enthusiasm will show, and others will be interested. These people are the best information channels in a company.
- People who do the day-to-day work on the problem being solved. They need to understand that the process is for them, not just for those who have more influence (or who they perceive as having more influence).

This group of people who are gathered together to work on a particular pilot should be organized as a "taskforce" or a "task team" that works together in an orderly fashion to perform the pilot project or solve a particular problem, then be disbanded. A new taskforce should be created to undertake the next pilot or solve the next problem. Some of the same people who served on earlier taskforces can serve on later ones, but new people should be added to broaden the program.

Some general guidelines for taskforces include:

1. *Group Size.* Each taskforce should have between five and ten people, enough to get the job done but not so many that the group dynamics become unwieldy.
2. *Membership.* Members should come from areas and functions involved in the change being implemented, with a majority from the shop floor. If one person must miss a meeting, an alternate must attend.
3. *Scheduling.* Groups should meet at least once every two

weeks, and more often at the beginning of the process. The meeting time should be consistent and predetermined so everyone can put it on their individual schedules.

4. *Time.* Meetings should be limited to a couple of hours so as not to interfere with other work people must perform. Most members will be doing this on top of a full work load. Other than planning or team building or education sessions, which take at least a full day, most of the work can be accomplished in this time frame.

5. *Accountability.* Each member has accountability to the team, and should realize the sacrifices involved in making and carrying out commitments within the team's scope of work.

6. *Documentation.* Meetings should follow written agendas, and minutes should be taken for distribution and future reference. Agendas should be separate from objectives; prep work should be sent one week before the meeting.

At the beginning of any taskforce's term, there must be some basic training in team building, as well as leadership training for the taskforce's project leaders. Techniques of structured problem solving should be taught, as well as team group dynamics and meeting management.

Just as the company must have a charter that sets out its agreement with the steering committee, the steering committee should have a basic taskforce charter that sets out its relationship with taskforces. The objectives of each taskforce must be set out and defined in a way that can be measured.

TASKFORCES[*]

The guidelines we offer our clients on taskforces are included below. Taskforces can serve as powerful management tools capable of accomplishing many simultaneous objectives. Some benefits include:

- Attention is focused on the importance of the issues the taskforce addresses.
- Resources can be temporarily concentrated to resolve an issue without disrupting day-to-day activities.
- The right people with the right skills and knowledge are brought together in a focused effort.
- A variety of groups can be represented through taskforce membership, including those whose commitment and support will be required for successful implementation.
- Decisions can be pushed deeper into the organization.

As always, the strengths of taskforces have within them the seeds of possible difficulties. A taskforce must be properly managed by both the taskforce leader and the steering committee if it is to avoid some common pitfalls, such as:

- Individual taskforce members from different parts of the organization having separate agendas.
- The temporary nature of the taskforce may limit members' willingness to commit personal time to it.

[*] Based on Edward J. Hay *The Just-in-Time Breakthrough: Implementing the New Manufacturing Basics* (New York: Wiley, 1988) pp. 201–202.

- Many nonmembers see the taskforce as implicit criticism of current practices and progress.

These and other pitfalls can be avoided if the right people are on the taskforce, if its process is properly planned, communicated, and managed by the steering committee, and if it has the leader's full support.

In addition, the right human resources people must stay involved with the pilot and problem-solving process. These are key support people who must get involved and stay involved. Their involvement with the OCA, and the knowledge they bring to the OCA with regard to understanding the people side of the survey, helps choose pilots and establish the training programs and seminars to supplement the pilots. They are the key people in documenting the skills gained in doing pilots and translating those gains into seminars that can help others understand the techniques and use them to solve problems in their own areas.

Their continued involvement with the pilot process will help them create the formal education programs that are necessary to educate the entire company about TQ and JIT. They also will use the information gained during the pilot process to help codify changes that will need to be made in the company's various systems in order to consolidate gains and push them forward.

The role of the leader in this phase is to stay informed and involved, but not as the primary driver. The leader can make sure this phase succeeds by working with the steering committee, sitting in on steering committee meetings, and generally monitoring progress, but such actions should be intended to help and not to direct.

The organization must believe that the leader still cares

about this effort. Therefore, the leader must stay visibly and emotionally involved.

At the same time, the organization must clearly display the power of TQ/JIT in the pilot phase—the first time at which TQ/JIT has become visible to much of the company's personnel. This pilot program should set a precedent so that when the company is ready to begin working with CIM the same process can be used.

Chapter 12

Formal Education

O nce the pilots are underway and the people directly involved with them are brought "up to speed" it is time to begin formal education of the entire workforce on the principles of and concepts behind Modern Integrated Manufacturing.

By this time, people should have been receiving formal communication, filtering down through the organization, about the company's work toward developing this new environment. They should have participated in the OCA, and should have been getting feedback about the results, the setting up of a steering committee, and the pilot projects that would be undertaken.

Many people will still be vague about the particulars of TQ and JIT. They need to be more formally and completely "educated."

The formal education of the entire workforce will take a very different form than the development of awareness in senior management. Middle managers, supervisors, and office and shop-floor workers by this time should have been exposed to the vision, read something on TQ/JIT/ CIM provided by the steering committee or project leader, heard the leader talk about why this is important and, ideally, discussed with him what the TQ/JIT effort should lead to.

A substantial awareness will be present and they will have either taken part in a pilot or seen or heard of one in action. The primary task of formal education is to provide additional organized information through seminars and workshops.

SEMINARS AND WORKSHOPS

Seminars should begin about two months into the pilot and problem-solving work.

After the first set of pilots is underway and the steering committee has time available, it should appoint a taskforce to organize the formal education program. This taskforce should have as members people who worked with the OCA, people from the training and development arm of the human resources department (one of whom should probably chair the taskforce), and others from various departments where special understanding of the work environment is necessary.

Members of the outside consulting organization (if one is being used) should also sit on this taskforce. In many instances, the consultants will conduct the first education courses. In any event, the consultants should not continue to deliver education courses, but should train insiders to do so. This instructor training component will deepen ownership and be a valuable training and development experience for those who become instructors. Something to note here is that it is very rare to find a consulting firm in TQ/JIT which also has ability to train employees to be instructors. Most simply package materials and try to teach some employees how to deliver those materials. There is a lot more to it than that! Don't let a technical consultant do this; it is a specialized job requiring special expertise.

This taskforce needs to replow a number of areas in order to develop proper courses with the proper emphasis. For example:

- It needs to dig into the OCA to find where people think they need the most help in changing things, where their perception of TQ and JIT is farthest from reality.

- It needs to go back to the benchmarking that has been done, but with an eye not to the companies that have solved the most problems, but the companies that do the best education (in many instances these will be the same companies). The taskforce should talk to people in these companies, explore with them how they conducted their educational programs, maybe observe some, and take whatever is useful information from them.
- The taskforce must go back to senior management and get them to rearticulate the vision as it was developed and as it has changed, if it has been at all tempered by reality in the last few weeks of running initial pilot projects.

After all this information has been gathered, the taskforce needs to draw up a list of workshops that should be given, and to whom. Education is an expensive process, both in terms of the cost of hiring the instructors (insiders or outsiders) and in terms of the time employees take from their regular work to attend formal education sessions.

Careful planning must be done so that the education programs have the least possible disruptive impact on work. For example, in some companies it might be less disruptive to run a seminar as a one-day, all-day affair and close a line or an office, while in others it may be impossible to do so and the seminar may have to be run in four late-afternoon sessions for two hours per session, even though this means asking people to stay two hours late four days and paying some overtime.

A system must also be designed so that people can attend the sessions most appropriate for their needs. Wherever possible, there should be a connection between professional development and the TQ/JIT sessions.

The specific population to attend depends a great deal on the situation in a particular company. Some commonly used guidelines include:

1. Courses everyone in the company may be asked to attend include:
   - A one-day mini-awareness session on Modern Integrated Manufacturing
   - Interpersonal Skills: 2–3 days
   - Principles of Total Quality and Just-in-Time: 3 days
2. Some courses that will be specially geared toward particular groups might include:
   - Problem solving, decision making, planning: 5 days
   - Total Quality, statistical process control techniques: 5 days
   - Managing change: 4 days
   - Total Quality for nonmanufacturing situations: 2 days
   - Influence skills: 2–3 days
   - Quality problem-solving tools: 2–5 days
   - Principles of pull systems: 1 day
   - Reducing set-up time: 1 day
   - JIT purchasing: 1 day
   - JIT in nonmanufacturing situations, supervisors: 2 days

Ideally, people should go through courses after they have participated in a pilot, but that will not always be the case. It might take years or at best months before everyone has been involved in one of the problem-solving efforts, and the formal education component to the planned change must serve as an engine to continue the process forward, especially for people who *have not* been involved in a pilot and are wondering if they ever will. This is another reason why the pilots that are done must be highly visible to everyone, and why the success of pilots must be communicated.

Classes should have no more than 25 attendees, and should disrupt regular work schedules as little as possible.

TEACHING ADULTS

It is commonly assumed that the techniques used to educate children are equally effective in training adults. People, therefore, have been recruited by companies to direct training and development activities based on their experience in teaching young people.

In addition, many managers, and even human resource people, assume that any educated and fairly organized person can do a good job at putting on a course or organizing an in-house education program.

The fact is that an adult is more than a grown-up child. An adult possesses characteristics as a learner that require different approaches than those that work with children.

When it comes to learning about the tools of TQ and JIT, a common premise must be challenged—that people will change their attitudes and behavior by closing gaps in knowledge. A whole segment of the training industry has developed since 1980 on the premise that by giving people more knowledge, they will somehow change the way they have operated for years and become oriented toward quality.

Traditional education was never intended to change attitudes and behavior, only to increase knowledge. Lecturing on a topic will rarely cause the listener to change behavior. Yet some companies continue to spend large sums thinking lectures will do just that.

How Adults Learn

Alfred North Whitehead said in 1931 that it was alright for educators to transmit knowledge as long as periods of major cultural change were greater than the periods of people's lives, so that what a person would learn as a youth would remain relatively valid throughout his or her lifetime. Whitehead then warned that: "We are living in the first period of human history where this assumption is false . . . today this time span is considerably shorter than that of human life, and accordingly . . . training must prepare individuals to face a novelty of conditions."

We are living today in a period of social and organizational change that is unprecedented, and TQ/JIT/CIM is accelerating the pace. Massive input of new knowledge, technological innovation, and new ways of working have resulted in people's jobs being eliminated, and the need for those people to be retrained.

In the past, changes less profound than those occurring today required a generation or more to take place, while today we expect them in a few months. The fact is that some of the knowledge one has when coming out of college is obsolete by the end of the first year on the job. What this points to is the reality of—and need for—lifelong learning.

Successful management trainers and organization development consultants have always understood that teaching adults is quite different from teaching children. Adults are almost always voluntary learners, and will simply leave or choose not to participate in a learning situation that does not meet their needs as they see them.

Much of this theory is drawn from Malcolm S. Knowles, who spent many years at Boston University. Knowles was an early leader in the training and development movement, as it grew after World War II and then blossomed into such outgrowths as the human potential movement and organization development.

Knowles and his colleagues articulated a number of assumptions that separate how adults learn from how children learn. These assumptions are adapted here to offer criteria for the development of MIM education. They are:

1. Adults want what they learn to be practical. They are facing problems that are getting in the way of their doing the job they set out to do, and they want to learn how to minimize, eliminate, or circumvent those problems so they can complete some task.
2. Adults have developed a self-concept of an independent being. They do not like to be protected and told what to do. When people in authority do protect or dictate, adults react in one of two ways: they become subservient because they do not believe they can do anything else, or they rebel either openly or in a covert way.
3. Adults want to use their experience in a learning situation to make both their experiences and the learning more relevant. Being told something worked in another company in another industry does not count; the adult reacts like a child who is told what worked in 1776. Today's

manager or hourly worker wants to hear about and learn about something he can easily relate to.

4. Adults want to take some of the responsibility for learning. Sitting and hearing a lecture is a noninvolving, one-way activity. It requires little of the learner other than keeping his eyes open. Real adult education includes ways to involve the learner actively through role plays, case studies, simulations, and games.

What all of this means is that if education in a MIM effort is going to succeed, it must meet a number of criteria:

- Tailored for relevance to the learner
- Designed to involve the learner as a partner in his education
- Focused on problems, tools, and techniques that are of concern now, not in the future
- Timed so that workshops, seminars, and other activities match the real-life work situations as they come up in the work process
- Conducive to adult interaction—open physical environment, nonclassroom setting, informal
- Responsive to what the learner has pointed out as his needs (by way of a formal needs assessment survey before formal education takes place)
- Allow the learner active involvement in planning his own learning.

As can probably be surmised by now, I am suggesting a format for the education phase that is quite different from what exists in most TQ/JIT/CIM efforts.

The necessity to have these conditions suggests, among

other things, that it is not good enough to take a soon-to-retire manager and give him a leader's guide on a TQ course and say "go learn this stuff and these slides." That may be okay if we want him to teach third graders (although it probably would not) but it certainly will not be effective with a group of adults. Companies that go this route are simply wasting money and actually setting the whole effort back rather than moving it forward.

TRAINING INSTRUCTORS

In some ways who teaches is as important as what is taught. In our mythical company of 3000 employees, it would be nearly impossible for the human resources people to find the time to instruct all of the courses to all of the people who must take them. That leaves aside the issue of whether the human resources people have the necessary technical competence to teach all of those courses. In almost all instances they do not.

Because of this, it is imperative that companies turn to outside consultants and trainers for a major part of their educational program. But the key is to use those outsiders to instill expertise in some group within the company so that the group can carry the education forward; in other words, the outsiders are hired to teach instructors, not merely to teach courses.

I prefer to train instructors for the courses everyone will take, and do the instructing myself for the courses that have more limited enrollment. To train instructors is often more expensive than to teach courses, especially as the number of people to go through each course gets smaller. For example, working with our 3000-person company it would probably cost about 20 percent more in the short run to hire Rath & Strong to train instructors to deliver the high-volume courses than it would to hire us to deliver all of the courses ourselves. But after that the curves should cross and it should be more economical to have insiders do the courses. I also think the rewards for the company would be worth the extra initial expense.

Training instructors is, in effect, conducting management development, especially when those instructors are drawn from the ranks of office workers, shop-floor personnel, or first-line supervisors. Training instructors creates much broader-based people who can continue to be catalysts for change in the future, and who can be tapped time and again as instructors or even internal consultants.

I also believe that having people as instructors who have "been there" enhances the learning experience for the course's participants. There is a somewhat intangible, but I believe very real, impact to having a first-line supervisor who has just come off the line go through a course taught by a former colleague who shows that he or she has a firm grasp of principles and communication skills.

People in organizations are much more willing to accept the kind of radical changes that are part of TQ and JIT if they do not believe it is being forced on them by outsiders or imposed on them by the top people in the organization.

Let us assume that there are three courses our mythical company wants everyone to go through. Each course should have two instructors delivering at one time. Therefore, for each of these three courses there will need to be three or four instructors prepared to deliver it. Because of a wash-out rate during the instructor-training process of about 40 percent, the company will need about 15 people to start the instructor process. These 40 percent will find that they are not good instructors, or they are uncomfortable speaking in groups, or they just do not want to make the time commitment to instructor training and future delivery of courses.

During the organization and early pilot phases, managers should scout the ranks of people they know for potential instructors. The sequence should go something like this:

1. The first step is for the instructor candidates to sit through a class taught by the outside consultant/trainer. During evenings and between sessions, this group should meet with the trainer to discuss what they heard and saw to better understand the trainer's rationale and approach.
2. Step two is ten days of intensive training for the group of instructors. This can be done in two five-day sessions, or in several segments of two or three days each.
3. Step three is for the candidates to co-instruct a session with the outside trainer.
4. Step four is for the candidates to instruct with the outside trainer observing from the back of the room and offering feedback following segments of the course.
5. The final step is certification.

The instructor-training program will include principles of teaching, interpersonal skills, influence skills, and exploring personal motivations and teaching styles.

The role of the leader in this phase must be to ensure that quality education aimed at adults takes place. If he has the right human resources people, his task will obviously be easier; if not, he had better get good outside help.

Chapter 13

Codification

Codification is the process of making the TQ and JIT gains permanent by changing the systems and norms the company lives by. There are five ways to do this:

1. Making sure the systems by which the company operates are consistent with the TQ/JIT philosophy.
2. Matching the yearly planning and budgeting process with TQ and JIT needs.
3. Ensuring the company's strategy is consistent with TQ and JIT.
4. Making permanent the advances made in management training and adult education.
5. Continuing the development of the company's climate and teamwork links between and among managers and other employees.

CENTRAL SYSTEMS

There are three systems that combine to form the company's central nervous system: the measurement system, the reward system, and the information system.

Simply put, what is measured and rewarded should conform to the principles of TQ and JIT, such as:

- Measuring quality
- Rewarding teamwork-oriented behavior
- Discouraging speed for internal efficiency
- Discouraging practices that perpetuate waste
- Measuring an action's impact throughout the system rather than in one small part of the process
- Measuring and rewarding "the right things done right the first time."

It may take five years to completely codify TQ/JIT gains, although the leader should begin thinking of this phase early in the process. But since TQ/JIT efforts in this country are for the most part in their infancy, there are few examples to cite of success in this difficult task.

However, there are examples of businesses that did not start the process early, and things fell apart. What I have seen happen is that for nine months of the year energy and attention are focused on innovation and experimentation in TQ and JIT. Then, usually in the fall, the annual budgeting process begins and people revert back into a sort of time warp to a pre-TQ/JIT era as they diagnose, crunch numbers, fill in formulae, and project for the CFO what might happen next year.

In most cases, this sort of exercise is, as one person once remarked, "akin to everyone lying to each other in great detail based on delusions of grandeur."

TQ and JIT will not become permanent until managers alter the targets they commit to achieve. The goal is to run a TQ/JIT business all the time, and make the TQ/JIT philosophy meld with the company's overall strategy.

Occasionally this will happen. Many companies—most large ones—have corporate strategies. When well done they establish direction for what products will be made, where they will be made, and what markets to pursue. Usually these plans are set independently of a TQ/JIT effort.

Let me give you an example of where the two efforts, overall strategy and developing a TQ/JIT environment, came together.

Rath and Strong began working in 1987 with a client who is also a client of a large strategy consulting firm, firm Y. The other firm and Rath and Strong have always enjoyed a friendship, but had never until this time worked together.

Rath & Strong was asked to spearhead a division-wide effort to revitalize manufacturing, while the strategy firm was asked to create a world-wide strategy. As is usually the case, the left hand did not know what the right was doing inside the corporation. The Rath & Strong client (the division) did not think what the strategy firm was doing had anything to do with our work, and the same was true of Y's client in the corporate office.

A senior partner of Y and I set up a meeting, with respective clients' knowledge, of strategy and operations consultants from our two firms, in order to share information and insight. It quickly became apparent that we had been correct in our assumption that there was significant overlap of our work, and what one was doing could have enormous impact on the other's work. By cooperating and sharing information, we would both be doing a better job for our clients.

Rath & Strong became the sort-of "general contractor" who, in addition to implementing JIT, integrated various manufacturing improvement programs and elements into one cohesive operational excellence strategy, while the other firm concentrated on questions of what businesses the company should be in, where product should be made, and make-or-buy decisions.

One of the big areas where coordination is necessary in such a case is for the two consultants to work with the same set of assumptions. In this case, the strategy firm was working under the assumption that what existed (current ways of thinking, current costs, efficiencies, capabilities, lead times, etc.) would remain more or less constant. Meanwhile, Rath

& Strong was getting ready to change the current operation by helping to dramatically reduce lead times, cut costs in the process, and generally improve capabilities.

The obvious danger was that we would be improving manufacturing and purchasing performance in a business that someone at the corporate level was deciding should be sold because of current cost structures. Momentous strategic actions were being contemplated that would cause the loss of many jobs and cause significant upheaval. These recommendations were made based on data and capabilities that TQ and JIT would change. By merging the two activities, the client received a much more complete and effective consulting effort.

This is just one example of the importance of insuring there is consistency and coordination between various development and strategy efforts.

MANAGEMENT DEVELOPMENT

Management development is a significant portion of the TQ/JIT effort. Closely connected is the continuation of teamwork and other climate-related elements.

Because of the reality of lifelong learning needs as part of a TQ/JIT effort, the human resources department must find ways to make permanent people-development efforts.

One aspect is to institutionalize the practice of training people to be internal consultants and setting them the task of being problem solvers and helpers on pilots, and instructors for workshops and seminars. High-potential people should be chosen, then required to spend 20 percent of their time on this, and membership in this group should rotate every 12–18 months.

Another way to solidify this area is to require new employees to go through basic teamwork skills training programs. At one client's business, the human resources director and I developed a team improvement workshop, a two-day program on the principles of teamwork and basic teamwork skills. At each workshop, groups of 15 newly hired people, or people who had not gone through the program for more than two years participated.

Another method of development is for managers to attend a team-building session along with the people who directly report to them. Rath & Strong's approach is called the Administrative Teambuilding Workshop (ATB). It is a fairly simple design that includes ways for the "natural work group" (manager and those who report to him) to define what ideal teamwork is for them, give and receive feedback, do cases and exercises, and establish goals for improvement. The result is the start of a teamwork atmosphere where barriers to interpersonal communication and cooperation are minimized or eliminated. When done on a company-wide scale, such workshops offer common experience and a common language. Once enough natural work groups participate, the teamwork thrust can be even more ingrained by cross-department team-building sessions.

Cross-department teamwork is even more important than intradepartment teamwork in a TQ/JIT effort because of the need for cooperation in problem solving and for information sharing. However, it is usually best to ensure teamwork within a department before tackling the more complex issues of relationships and cooperation between departments. At the appropriate time, cross-department teamwork sessions should be conducted to improve understanding and communication between people who must depend on each other across department lines.

Deepening gains also requires standardizing the practices and tools that helped achieve those gains. More than just setting standards, measuring, and rewarding accordingly, it requires that people be committed to a way of doing things that will bring consistent results. This will not happen by telling people to do it, or promising to pay them more. It will only happen if they want to operate that way. They must believe in the new way of operating and they must feel they will derive something beneficial from operating that way.

All of our climate survey work over the last ten years has shown that hourly workers care deeply about making quality products, in many cases more deeply than anyone at any other level of the organization. What they produce is tied to their self-image. This should be heartening news; it is the kind of an association between worker and product that should point to a ready acceptance of ways to improve. What must complement that sense of acceptance, though, are reward and measurement systems that reflect and support movement in the right direction.

STRUCTURE FOR CODIFICATION

The steering committee should put together another task-force, on systems and norms, chaired by the leader with members being the top people from the human resources department as well as industrial engineering, management information systems, and finance departments. Again, these should be people with as little stake as possible in maintaining the status quo. This is often easier said than done since many of these people's jobs seem closely tied to administering current systems. In fact, we have found that the people most resistant to change are middle managers with such specialized staff jobs. It is up to the leader to choose the right people for the job. They need to be analytical people who can determine what needs to be eliminated, modified, and added to make the messages sent about how the company works conform to the new vision.

This taskforce needs to analyze the current measurement, reward, and information systems to see which ones will possibly hinder the company in meeting the vision of what the company should be like in a TQ/JIT environment. Again, a close reading of the Opportunity and Climate Assessment results will give the taskforce a sense of what issues are important.

At this stage, the leader must provide judicious leadership to the taskforce. He or she has to make sure that the continued rethinking of strategy and the ongoing budget process take into account TQ and JIT.

CHANGING THE DAY-TO-DAY BUSINESS

From decisions made about codifying these changes will come the adaptation of or creation of new systems, which may lead to a new set of values and norms and to activities that conform with the articulated vision. If this is not done, and done carefully, companies will never really be able to "institutionalize" the gains that can be made with TQ and JIT.

I have seen companies years into a TQ/JIT effort say they have educated literally thousands of people, but that the company still operates day-to-day in much the same way it always has. The budgeting cycle still asks for short-term numbers and still looks like it did before the company was into TQ and JIT, except there is more money budgeted for more education and more consulting time to run more pilots. And the same quality problems exist as existed before anyone ever heard of TQ. This should *not* be allowed to happen.

CHANGE MEASUREMENTS FIRST

The most important system to change is the measurement system. From changes in measurement come changes in rewards. The easiest system to change is the information system, but again, that cannot be changed until it is determined what will be measured.

System change is never easy, and the leader must make sure it is worth the effort before embarking on such a task. The rationale to do it goes something like this: Customers are demanding different performance from suppliers today. Performance is based on systems and certain ways of doing business. These ways of doing business are tracked by measures reflected in the measurement and reward systems. If ways of doing business must change then the measures of how to track that performance should change. This in turn implies change in the way people act.

The basic measurement and reward system will have a major impact on the company's norms, the often unspoken rules of decorum or "rules of the road" that govern how people go about their daily work lives.

The measurement and reward system determines who will get promoted, what will be stressed, and the basis on which people will get raises, bonuses, and other rewards.

The marketplace demands results that can be achieved best by companies doing business in a TQ/JIT environment. In order to do business in a TQ/JIT environment, many companies must change the norms that form the basis of the behavior of managers and other employees and that means a change in how performance is measured.

Two examples come to mind quickly. One is purchasing, the other is cost accounting. In traditional purchasing departments, the outlook has always been that a company had to have as many fall-back positions as possible. The idea was that suppliers, if given the chance, would likely take advantage of customers, and/or that Murphy's Law dominated thinking and said that there must be multiple sources of supply because something was bound to go wrong. The result was that customers had to have many suppliers.

What this attitude brought about, however well meaning, was a system that is complicated and somewhat difficult to manage, and that often results in contentious relationships, not trusting ones where vendor loyalty is prized.

The new purchasing philosophy calls for collaboration with vendors. The idea that makes up the essence of JIT purchasing is to have a long-term, mutually beneficial relationship with fewer but better suppliers. The argument is that being cut-throat runs both ways, that if suppliers are always afraid that this may be their last meal, they may not be giving a customer all that the customer needs and wants. The customer needs to take responsibility for ending the vicious purchasing cycle: "Hold on, let's set up a system where we learn to trust each other, where I can tell you 'you are my supplier on this item' and you can tell me 'I guarantee you X amount of that item when you need it.'"

There is enormous waste in the purchasing end of most businesses. Much of this waste can be eliminated through setting up a procurement system that measures quality in a different way, and where the norms of the purchaser/vendor relationship are far different than in the traditional relationship.

The second example is in cost accounting. There are a number of cost-accounting measurements that are not necessary in a TQ/JIT environment because they are either meaningless or antithetical to the environment and therefore detrimental to TQ/JIT taking hold. Six of them are:

- Machine utilization
- Direct and indirect labor ratios
- Overhead ratios
- Measuring speed
- Set-up and run times
- Cost per purchase order

Machine Utilization: The only time this is a valid measurement in a JIT environment is as a measure of capacity when a company is trying to decide whether or not to buy more equipment. It is inappropriate when it encourages machines to be running when product is not needed, resulting only in inventory.

Direct and Indirect Labor Ratios: The proper use of this measure is to keep direct and indirect labor in proper relation in times when volumes are changing but methods are staying the same. It is therefore not appropriate to use when changing methods in a TQ/JIT effort.

Overhead Ratios: Most cost-accounting systems believe that direct labor is measurable and identifiable, but that indirect labor and overhead are not measurable, and therefore get out of hand unless they are handcuffed in a direct relationship with direct labor. If a TQ/JIT effort reduces both labor and material costs, that hurts the overhead ratio, so a company can reduce total cost but still not have positive results according to this ratio. For example, if the typical cost breakdown for a $10 item is:

$ 7	material
1	labor
2	overhead
$10	

The overhead is 20 percent. If, after a successful TQ/JIT implementation the cost has decreased to $7.50, the breakdown is:

$ 5	material
0.50	labor
2	overhead
$ 7.50	

the overhead is 27 percent.

Measuring Speed: Speed—often measured as pieces per hour—is completely anathema to the JIT philosophy where the goal is to produce enough to meet customer requirements.

Set-up and Run Time: Having ratios of set-up to run sends a message that run time is good and set-up time is bad. But this measurement resists the JIT requirement that reduced set-up times be reinvested in more frequent set-ups and reduced lot sizes.

Cost per Purchase Order: Again, this measurement had an original purpose of controlling changes in volume on the assumption that methods will stay the same. The cost-per-purchase order measurement says blanket orders and systems contracting are bad, but JIT purchasing says exactly the opposite.

It is important to clarify here that a TQ/JIT manufacturing philosophy is not inconsistent with the principles of cost accounting. It is true that several of the traditionally held measures of cost accounting and how they are interpreted would need to change in a TQ/JIT environment.

Often the best way to approach these sorts of systems change is for the leader to charter a taskforce to look into what needs to change and make recommendations as to how those changes should take place. Then pilot efforts should start to begin the process of making gains permanent.

CLOSING THE LOOP, BEGINNING ANEW

Another role of the leader in the codification of the TQ/JIT environment is to start the process of rethinking the business strategy. This will probably be done after about a year of the pilot/problem solving phase and well into the phase of formal education.

It may be that the strategy of the business will not need to be altered in any way with the adoption of a TQ/JIT strategy, that TQ/JIT and eventually CIM are the pathways to achieve the existing strategy. On the other hand the leader may need to spearhead an effort to devise a new strategy, a refined vision that will act like a second-stage booster rocket to give the company the lift it needs to get out of the atmosphere and capture new market share.

This is a good time to begin thinking about CIM, now that the company is on the way to establishing a solid base of TQ and JIT. At this point, the company should have a clear idea of what kinds of activities can be eliminated, which systems will be dropped in the future, and which parts of the business could benefit from the automation and information support provided by CIM.

The first two years of the TQ/JIT/CIM effort might form an era, and toward the end of that era the leader must begin to prepare both himself and the company for the next one.

Perhaps the three biggest questions before the leader after the first couple of years of the TQ/JIT effort are:

1. How can we sustain what we have achieved, given rapid changes in the market place and internal changes?
2. How can we leverage what we have accomplished so far so that we can continue to achieve more impressive gains than we achieved in the pilots?
3. How can we deepen the commitment to change of the people who have been involved, and capture the imagination of people who have so far not been involved?

These issues of sustainability and broadening are ones the leader must ensure that the top team grapples with. In doing so, they must leave open lines of communication and involvement so that other people are contributing to the answers.

There are not any universal answers to these three questions. What is right for one company and one leader is not necessarily the answer for another. The trick to winning this game is for the leader to create the climate where such questions are addressed by the right people in his organization. If the leader poses the questions to the right people, sets an environment of trust and openness where only problems and not people are attacked, and establishes the right standards, such questions will be answered.

From my own experience and from that of my clients who have worked hard at answering these questions, I offer some thoughts—call them "Ciampa's Seven Rules of Sustainability"—for the leader who has gotten an organizational excellence effort started and wants to ensure it keeps going with commitment and enthusiasm but without the leader having to push the effort along each step of the way.

1. *Take your own medicine.* Do not expect people to participate fully in a change effort unless they see you doing the same. Attend education sessions, use the techniques and tools of TQ/JIT, and do it visibly. When there are delivery problems that bubble up to your level, have them charted and use Pareto analysis to identify root causes. If teambuilding is a major thrust in your company's effort, make sure you and your staff have gone through a teambuilding session, and not just in a perfunctory way.

2. *Be consistent.* Just as the old saying in sales is true, selling starts when the customer says "no," it is also true that commitment to TQ/JIT/CIM begins when things are not going well. If TQ/JIT/CIM is good only in "up times," it is not worth the trouble. Stick to the path and use the tools in down periods as well as when business is up, and avoid the temptation to revert to old ways if business gets slow.

3. *Be a model for what you want others to do.* The surest way to lose people's attention and enthusiasm is to say

one thing at one point and months later do another. People will judge what you really expect and how serious you are based on what you do, not on what you say verbally, in memos, or in the annual report; their judgment will be particularly harsh after the initial flurry of activity and once the TQ/JIT effort settles somewhat.

4. *Make sure key managers are playing the same game and using the same play book.* If employees see you saying and doing one thing and managers acting in other ways or saying other things, they will see the TQ/JIT effort as just another program. This is particularly crucial as the effort moves down through the organization and mid-level managers take on more responsibility. Also, make sure roles are defined. Your managers should pay special attention to role definition as pilots and formal education proceed.

5. *Understand that you are dealing with a general system that is made up of a number of interactive parts.* Changing one piece of the system will have an effect on the others. Your role is to maintain balance while moving forward, and the other members of the top team must communicate often and well to ensure what is happening in their departments or groups is understood by others who may be affected.

6. *Make sure all departments participate in the TQ/JIT effort.* These tools and techniques work best when everyone is pulling in the same direction. At the same time it is important to let departments move at a pace that meets their needs—the point here is that that movement forward should not be significantly out of synch. Achieving the right balance is a top team task.

7. Above all, understand that the opportunities that are so seductive can only be brought about under a culture where people are going out of their way to improve what is around them all the time, and trying to make things better. *Creating such a culture is one of the few things a leader cannot delegate.* It is not easy to develop this culture, and it cannot be done quickly. Doing the job requires a vision of how things could work and a carefully thought-through yet flexible plan. It also requires enormous patience, perseverance, and confidence in yourself and the rest of your organization.

TQ, JIT, and CIM can combine to solve the problems facing manufacturing today. The tools and techniques are there, and they have been tested. The real trick is to make them work. That task falls squarely on the shoulders of the leader. This is the leader's challenge.

Index

Index

Index

Index